Asfidity and Mad-Stones

A Further Ramble Through Hillfolks' Hoodoo

H. Byron Ballard

Smith Bridge Press

Asheville, NC

Asfidity and Mad-Stones: A Further Ramble Through Hillfolks' Hoodoo

© 2015 H. Byron Ballard, Asheville, NC

www.myvillagewitch.com

Edited by D.A. Sarac
Cover Design by Diotima Mantineia
Author photo by Machaela Treadway
Appalachia Rise by the Author

ISBN 978-0-9967583-0-7

Produced in the United States of America
Smith Bridge Press
Asheville, NC
SmithBridgePress@gmail.com

The spirits are alive, magic is afoot, and the cherry bark cough syrup is ready. In the hilltops of Appalachia, Byron Ballard is showing us how it's done! This book is indeed a rare gem for those hungry to learn about surviving folk traditions and practical magic. Byron reveals what it is like to be a village witch by transforming the everyday into avenues for magic and reflection while offering insight, stories, history, lore, and rabbit trails galore with her usual cunning charm, attitude, humor, and grace. If you have yet to have the pleasure of learning from her in person, here is the next best thing because this book is pure Ballard!

- Chris Orapello, Pagan artist and podcaster

I have such a deep appreciation for Byron's commitment to keeping the magical ways of the Appalachian Hill-Folk alive. It is in the land, the family, the heart and soul. It is coal, lard, strings, song, prayer, herb, token, dung and jar. It is in the kitchen, the graveyard, the old oak and the cellar. It is so simple it can be missed and so deep we fall into it. It calls the heart home. *Asfidity and Mad-Stones* is a rich invitation into a culture too often overlooked and minimized for its wisdom and power. These are her people, my people... our blood and bones. Our folks have deep magic that romances the land, courts the haint and bells the dame and, if lost....something sacred in the human soul will be lost. In the storytelling tradition of the hills, she rolls her words out like a red carpet drawing us all into Laurel Groves and Haunted Coves. My Shenandoah Ancestors rise and applaud this book!

-Orion Foxwood, author of *The Candle and the Crossroads*

This is a book about magic grounded in place, about ancestral magic made new, about magic that the common people use. Muriel Rukeyser said that, "In time of crisis, we summon up our strength. Then, if we are lucky, we are able to call every resource, every forgotten image that can leap to our quickening, every memory that can make us know our power. And this luck is more than it seems to be: it depends on the long preparation of the self to be used." Byron's book, written in what she has aptly dubbed "Tower Time," is a guidebook to the calling up of resources and forgotten images that can help us to know our power. Reading it is an act of preparation.

-Hecate Demetersdatter-Blogger, wise woman

Have you ever wanted to root your magical practice more deeply in your everyday life? Some of us weren't lucky enough to learn folk magic at our granny's apron strings, but H. Byron Ballard makes up for our impoverishment in *Asfidity and Mad-Stones*, an insightful guidebook to North Carolina hillfolks' hoodoo and magical lore. With both book learning and common sense, Byron has given us a superb guide to the magical lore of the land she holds supremely dear. At a time when most of the world has forgotten that all land is hallowed land, Byron teaches us to root our magic and spirituality in the everyday practices of life once again. Hail to the Ancestors, may Appalachia rise!

-Caroline Kenner-Washington Witchdoctor, healer and owner
of The Fool's Dog Tarot Company

Asfidity and Mad-Stones is not just an entrancing collection of remembered folklore from a rapidly-disappearing culture carved out of ancient mountains by a tough, determined, and ingenious people — though it is that. Nor is it just a book of clear magical teachings and magical spells — though it is that, as well. What sets this book apart is the voice of its author — a Witch who stands firmly rooted in the land and traditions of her Ancestors, looks with fearless clarity into the future, and carefully assesses what needs to be done in the present to shift and change what is to come. Then...and this is important...she actually does the work. The book is an inspiration and an exhortation to do the work ourselves, to weave threads of remembered magic into our own, with gratitude and respect for those who have kept the skills and knowledge alive through the centuries. It is a book that strengthens the fabric of magic in our lives with intelligence, insight and captivating prose. And for that gift, I am very, very grateful.

-Diotima Mantineia-
Chief Stargazer at Urania's Well Astrology

Grab your work-basket and a good, sharp blade, and come along in to the back lots, the meadows, the hills. Byron shows us the folkways of her beloved Appalachian homeland, and shares practical wisdom and workings that she has learned and adapted over a lifetime of practice. Ms. Ballard tells of Ancestors and ghosts, folk-sayings and omens. She offers up a list of herbal helpers, discusses fundamental needs, and shares all manner of works - from blessings to banes. All while weaving an enchanting picture of the land and the spirit of place that holds her heart. This is good, get-dirt-under-your-nails craft. By the time you are finished reading this charming book, you should have an impressive toolkit of local plants, dirt, stones, and waters, and a bit of a sore back. Dig in deep to this gem, and be sure to carry a buckeye in your pocket, encourage plantain in your yard, mind your dishwater, and pay attention to the moon.

-Jen (Rue) Holmes, Blogger, Herb Mistress,
Cat-herder at Rue and Hyssop

Welcome back to the magical world of folk lore, natural magic, herbal healing and mystery. Byron's first book was just a taste of the Hillfolks Hoodoo universe, now you get a full and satisfying meal. This book is priceless if you want to know the secrets of folk magic from an expert who has spent years collecting the stories and recipes. From the first words of "Appalachia Rise" to the last sentence, you will feel yourself sinking into a world of magic like none other. Step into Byron's sphere...if you dare.

-Tish Owen-
Author of Chasing the Rainbow and Spell it Correctly

Once again, Byron Ballard walks us through the contemporary uses of mountain hoodoo with respect, common sense, and historical appreciation. If this is your path, you won't find a better guide.

-Alex Bledsoe, author of the Tufa novels

Drawing on an older wisdom passed down through generations of the people of Appalachia, Byron Ballad reveals more of the practical workings and pragmatic magic that fuel the renewed appeal of Hillsfolk Hoodoo. More than a tutorial, this latest book is an often playful and witty guide to the earthy common sense rootwork of everyday folks. Continuing the thread begun in *Staubs and Ditchwater*, Byron weaves the results of her latest research into the fascinating mesh of knowledge where cures and abeyances, juice and dust, become not simply parts of another magical system but rather are integrated into another way of being human and helpful in the places where we live and work.

Adding to the pleasure of this exploration of Appalachian folkways, hoodoo and rootwork, Byron shares personal stories of local haints, haunts and the relationships forged between workers and the spirits that roam these wild places. *Asfidity and Mad-Stones* is a book of remembrance surely, but it is also one of resonance. Put this one next to your work-basket because you will want to refer to it again and again.

-Wren Walker, the Witches' Voice

Special thanks to my readers and the lovely people who said such lovely things. So much love to Lisa and Kim of the Raven and Crone for their support and encouragement in all things witchery. Gratitude and Big Love to Elinor, Fox, Mischa (and Mr. Mole), to La Laity and Mark Walker at the Clep Bar, to Maranda and Gary and the boys (Women's Institute next time?). Blessings on Annie Sarac partner in crime and Editor Extraordinaire. And thanks for the Neolithic tour of Fife, young Terry Doherty.

This book is dedicated to Dena Boyd Randall, Uncle Ted White, Dorothy Morrison, and Star Bustamonte (for driving Miss Crazy). And to the Taureans: Betty, Evvie, Joe, Kate and Ben.

Parts of this book were developed as an online folk magic curriculum and I am grateful to all the students who participated in it. You know who you are.

Let Appalachia rise.

I believe in the justice of the Ancestors.

I believe in the wisdom of the hills and hollers.

I believe in the strength of the mountaineers.

Let Appalachia rise!

I swear by my granny's apron.

I swear by the cool sweet water.

I swear by the blood of my people.

Let Appalachia rise.

Let Appalachia rise!

Contents

Asfidity and Mad-Stones

Foreword

On a hot July evening with a Blue Moon on the rise and crickets making mad music outside my window, I settled in to read an early copy of Byron's latest, Asfidity and Mad-Stones. And oh! what a pleasure it was. Her voice comes through with such clarity that I find myself feeling that she's sitting at my side – a friendly witch come to visit. When she begins to speak of the necessity of familiarizing ourselves with the particular bit of "hallowed ground" we inhabit, I grin in recognition, remembering my total immersion into learning the flora, fauna, and folkways of this adopted home of mine. Books and neighbors and keeping my eyes open helped a lot but, forty years on, I'm still learning and Byron is one of my most honored teachers. When I dare to incorporate Appalachian magic into my novels, I look to Byron to help me get it right.

This magical place we call Western North Carolina cast its spell on me from the beginning. I learned from my neighbors about scheduling not only gardening but also almost any activity on the farm according to the moon signs and The Old Farmer's Almanac. Louise, down the mountain, made me soon aware of the importance of staying out of the cucumbers and not making kraut when my period was 'on me.' She showed me how to make a powder from a dirt dauber's nest, a powder that cleared up my son's stubborn diaper rash overnight. And another neighbor left me momentarily dumbfounded when she called in great agitation telling me to come quick and read the verses from the Bible that would stop her husband's nosebleed.

I went, I read, and the bleeding stopped. If I'd had this book back then, I wouldn't have been so puzzled.

And what a glorious mélange of folk wisdom, nature lore, mother wit, and just plain good storytelling this little book is! It really is like sitting on the front porch with a friendly witch, sipping iced tea and learning what it means when your left ear itches or how to use dirty dishwater for a hex.

If you seem hesitant about all this talk of magic, the witch leans back in her rocker and reminds you that "children grow up with a belief in magic that is fueled . . . by a certainty that the world is more than it seems" and, shooting you a long, knowing look, she promises "practicing these simple magics affords you a chance to return to this place of wonder, where mystery is an always-sweet puzzle and there is adventure and delight."

You trust this friendly witch and as you hear more of her family's handed-down teachings and the accumulation of years of practice, you lean back, relax, and listen, led into that place of wonder. She tells you of candle magic and the use of various dusts, of chicken feet and Reese's cups, and she delves into the glorious pharmacopeia of our mountain plants. Witch hazel, elderberry, chickweed and dandelion, plantain and mugwort, mint and 'sang – even the names are a healing song.

You are surprised to realize that evening is drawing on – how long have you been sitting here listening to these wonderful tellings? You excuse yourself and go into the house, returning with little glasses, a plate of shortbread, and a 'drop of the creature.' Anything to keep the flood of wisdom flowing.

Accepting your offering, the friendly witch moves on to practical magic – from dealing with burns to politely clearing a house of lingering haints. The tinctures and hexes, omens and admonitions she shares are drawn mainly from Appalachian tradition but with a sprinkling of items 'borried' from other cultures. And in the liminal time between day and night, as the full moon rises over the mountain, the friendly witch has stories to tell of hauntings and cleansings, and she talks with reverence and affection of the Little People who share the land.

She's right good company, this friendly witch, and when at last you must say goodbye to her, your head is spinning, filled to the brim with receipts and charms, hexes, hoodoos, and workings of all sorts – a veritable cornucopia of folk wisdom.

You'll be glad you have this little book to consult, should you forget the words of the burn charm or should the exact sequence of belling and anointing the house slip your memory. And with the book, you can summon Byron to come sit at your side again and once more delight you with the wisdom of The Ancestors.

Vicki Lane
Wool Branch Farm
July 31, 2015

Introduction

Into a Laurel Hell

In the years since the publication of my first book on Appalachian folk magic, I have toured and talked more than I ever would have thought. I have also been teaching an online course in advanced techniques largely made up by people who read that first book and were ready for more. Lucky for me—and I hope, for you—all this traveling and talking has afforded me more places to learn how others practice these old and odd remnants of a time gone by.

Or has it?

That has been one of the real joys of all that talk—I have discovered there are many more repositories of all this knowledge. Sometimes it survives in family stories and traditions. It often survives in little sweet pieces—like the grandma who always saved bits of broken glass and put them in a large Mason jar in the kitchen window. When I started writing down the things I remembered from growing up in a cove in the western part of this big old county, I never thought I'd get to the place where I was speaking at conferences and festivals, signing books, and learning more every day about this set of practices.

But I did and I have and I continue to build on the skeletal framework of my memory as I go my ways. One of the chief delights of all this travel has been talking to folks whose families have different traditions and I again wonder how much of this has been passed down as family stories and isn't lost at all. I give you the story of the mad-stone, as an example. That's where the name of this new book came from, after all.

I was doing a book event in Black Mountain and someone in the audience asked me if I'd ever heard of a "mad-stone." A mad-stone! My mind went immediately back to my childhood. I was hanging around some family members at some gathering or other and a group of men were gossiping about one of the younger ones who wasn't around. He keeps chasing tail like that and that boy better have a mad-stone in his pocket. I wasn't allowed to know about it and forgot about it until that very moment. You will see a discussion of the use of mad-stones in Chapter Ten, in case your curiosity (like mine) gets the better of you.

Staubs and Ditchwater was a primer — an introduction to Appalachian folk magic as I practice it and to the culture that surrounds me as a writer and as Asheville's "village witch." But a primer is only a sip of all there is to know about these old practices. As I lead workshops, teach classes, and lecture on this "hillfolks' hoodoo," I learn more stories and materials and techniques. And as I continue to practice my craft, I develop new ways of doing what needs to be done and I become braver about trying new ideas.

When I stepped into the world of folk magic practitioners, I also began to compare notes with folks in very different traditions and cultures. Each encounter adds to my stock of materials and techniques. Doing lectures, conferences, and book events has allowed me to meet people who shared some of the ways of their Gone Before people and I learned more that way, too. I have marveled at how generous people are with their stories and then I remember that we are a tribe of tellers here in the mountains and we like nothing more than sharing a story.

My spiritual path is different from many of my tribe, however, and I walk that fence-rail as carefully as I can. I have discovered that many people are willing to overlook my religious stuff and see me as one of them. Others are not so free to let me be and I respect them for holding fast to what they know. One of the virtues of mountain folks has always been a canny ability to mind our own business and we are mostly good about that, even in matters of religion.

This book, then, is the result of new experiences, cross-pollination with other people who do what I do, as well as a desire to go deeper into the world of Appalachian folk magic. It is a breathless and sometimes darksome place and that puts me in mind of a laurel hell.

The cove where I grew up had been logged and was logged again when I was in junior high school. The mountain above had also been used to pasture cattle for many years, which is what gave it its common name, Old Baldy. There weren't many wild and untouched areas on our mountain so I was never warned about those tricky old laurel hells until much later in life.

Mountain Laurel (kalmia latifolia) grows into scraggly tangled groves that are almost impossible to navigate if you wander into them unprepared. They are dark and cool looking on a hot summer afternoon and there are always inviting trails that enter the tangle on all sides— animal trails mostly, but some are natural breaks in the vegetation. They are, at the heart of it, deceptively beautiful and potentially dangerous. You can navigate a laurel hell if you know its ways and keep your wits about you.

Here's what Horace Kephart (in his wonderful 1906 "Camping and Woodcraft") had to say about laurel hells:

> *A canebrake is bad enough, but it is not so bad as those great tracts of rhododendron, which cover mile after mile of steep mountainside where few men have ever been. The natives*

call such wastes "laurel slicks," "woolly heads," "lettuce beds," "yaller patches," and "hells." The rhododendron is worse than laurel, because it is more stunted and grows more densely, so that it is quite impossible to make a way through it without cutting, foot by foot; and the wood is very tough.

Two powerful mountaineers starting from the Tennessee side to cross the Smokies were misdirected and proceeded up the slope of Devil's Court House, just east of Thunderhead. They were two days in making the ascent, a matter of three or four miles, notwithstanding that they could see out all the time and pursued the shortest possible course. I asked one of them how they had managed to crawl through the thicket. "We couldn't crawl," he replied, "we swum," meaning they had sprawled and floundered over the top.

These men were not lost at all. In a "bad laurel" (heavily timbered), not far from this, an old hunter and trapper who was born and bred in these mountains, was lost for three days, although the maze was not more than a mile square. His account of it gave it the name that it bears today, "Huggins's Hell."

See how you could crawl around in the humid, gnat-infested interior, where the filtered light gives it a peculiar underwater feel, for hours or even days before you happen on a track that leads out and into the fresh mountain air? Plenty of local tales feature hapless victims who wander (often under the influence of strong drink) into the laurel, into a bad hell, never to be seen or heard from again.

Going more deeply into hillfolks' hoodoo won't be deceptive or potentially dangerous, but we will be exploring some new protocols, enhanced materials, and tricky ethical constructs. We'll hold true to the notion from *Staubs* that attitude is everything, we will continue to embrace the joy of discovery, and we will dig even further into these old—and sometimes new— ways. But we'll make sure we know how to navigate through the grove and to get ourselves back home in time for supper.

A word to the wise regarding hatefulness and backbiting.

Rising above the fray—isn't that an interesting expression? As you start to stretch your wings and let people know what you're up to with your folk magic practice, you are likely to join all sorts of online forums and discussion groups. Your experience in the large and diverse world of hoodoo and rootwork will put you into contact with people of varying levels of experience, as well as different approaches to social interactions. These forums sometimes erupt into nasty backbiting and trash talk, often about people who aren't part of the group. My unsolicited advice on that is the first line of this paragraph: rise above the fray. Keep your own counsel. You don't need to leave the group, but you may want to hold yourself in silence as the silliness progresses. It probably won't help to try to be the voice of reason and it may make you a new and handy target. As the mountaineers did with that old hell, swim above it and keep going where your curiosity leads you.

There is something about this work—so close to the earth and so connected to the world of spirits—that brings out the best and the worst in people. Try to keep your heart clear, your eyes open, and your common sense close by and you'll be well served. There are lots of good ideas and interesting experiences that can be gleaned from these encounters, by the way.

And a thick laurel hell is a liminal place, an in-between space where almost anything can happen. We are likely to run into wild creatures and folks that we can't quite see, but are our relatives that have gone on. We will figure out how to treat with and entice the spirits of the old land beneath our feet.

As long as you remember—attitude is everything!

Got your work-basket and some fresh spring water to drink? Let's explore this old hell and see what we find.

We will be sating our curiosity with a little bit of history, of lore about this particular set of cultures, ethics for use of magic, techniques for accessing energies, tools, materials, practical common sense, development of helpful products like special waters and smokes, gathering and wildcrafting, study of the Five Needs, and some handy receipts scattered throughout.

Shoo, that's a lot to cover. We'd best get on with it.

*Count all the morning fogs of August
and you will know how many snows there will be
come winter.*

Chapter One

Living on Hallowed Land

As I sit here, typing this up for you and thinking about these next weeks, I can turn to my right and see the French Broad River winding its way northward through the old industrial heart of Asheville. This lifelong friend is the third oldest river in the world, older even than this chain of mountains. Only the New River and the Nile are older. The Tsalagi people called this section of the river "Tahkeeostie," which loosely translates as "racing waters."

This little river snakes through the oldest mountains in the world. That's all...the oldest. So if you are from this place or you visit this place, you will be seduced by the layers of life and experience that permeate everything here. The earth energies here, which, of course, include the way the water flows and the land shifts and the critters migrate—are low and steady and very, very strong. Unlike human beings, the land gets stronger, its energy more powerful, as age and experience weave into it. People are called into this area and they get wrapped up in power places and vortices and such...but they often fail to notice the deep, low, almost-audible hum of the land itself.

We talk about concepts of sacred space and speak of cemeteries and places where tragedies happened as "hallowed ground." From a human point-of-view, those places have special significance because of our history and connection to them.

I challenge you to consider all of it—the whole great ball of the Earth—as sacred space and holy ground. When you hear places in the Middle East referred to as The Holy Land, I invite you to nod your head sagely and think to yourself—buddy, it is all holy land. The pretty park down the road from your house, the wild spaces of Australia, the melting icecaps, removed mountains—all of it holy, all of it sacred, all of it worth consideration and worth fighting for.

We live in a terribly mobile time. Most people don't live in the town they were born in and many people travel regularly because of the professions they have chosen. It can make it hard to think of a particular piece of land as your land.

Coming into a deep relationship with the land around you is easier when you are settled there, and almost painful when you and your blood relations have been in a particular part of the world for many generations.

My roots in this particular place—in the southern highlands of Appalachia—are deep and twisty, and I hope I may be forgiven if I sometimes take that for granted in our multi-modal and migratory culture. If you are someone who continues to live in or near the place you were born, you have an odd connection into that land, whether intentional or not. We're going to look at some ways to forge or deepen your connections to the land whether you are a native, an incomer, a country-person, or an urban dweller.

The "back to the land" movement of the 1960s and 1970s saw a generation of idealists and dreamers attempt to return to a pre-Industrial Age lifestyle. Much of the modern movement in animal husbandry, land management, and herbal medicine, grew from their dedication and the trial-and-error techniques for reclaiming an older lifestyle. That movement was itself built, in part, on the tough resilience of the generations that survived the Great Depression. That, in turn, harkened back, in southern Appalachia at least, to the migration from subsistence farming to the mill villages of the industrial Southland.

So, you see, there are stepping-stones back to where we want to be. And we have the advantage of knowledge our Ancestors didn't have—a Web full of useful information—if we sometimes lack our Forebears' determination and courage. Our work-basket has a few more sharp tools to add to the ones our great-grandmothers passed down.

You will read that word throughout this book—work-basket—and a wee explanation here may help you along. Many women of a certain generation and class kept a work-basket or sewing basket. It is an enclosed basket of medium size, sometimes with a Bakelite or bone handle, sometimes not. My work-basket is round and dark red and the top of it is completely removable and sports a cocoa-colored satin tassel that is strung through with a greenish bead and a "Chinese" coin with a square hole in the middle.

I see work-baskets at thrift stores and sometimes I buy them. They are sweet and terribly sad, affording me a glimpse into the past and painting a portrait of a woman I didn't know. Inside sets a bit of unfinished tatting, wooden spools with cotton thread, scissors shaped like a stork, odd buttons, a folded paper that holds needles, a silver needle threader, a pincushion shaped like a tomato with an emery-filled strawberry dangling from a braided thread.

As we gather more information and learn more techniques, I invite you to assemble your own work-basket—literal or virtual—to catch the oddments we collect along this journey.

Let's step lightly now into this long-term land relationship. Start with knowing where you are. What's the geography? Do you live by the sea, in the high desert, in the middle of a great city? How many seasons do you have and how long do they last? What is your FDA planting zone? What animals and plants are natives there and who lived on the land before you?

Years ago, I was digging potatoes in the same garden I had planted as a young woman with my daddy, a tender act of ultimately impossible reclamation. My hoe struck a small stone and I bent to throw it to the side of the field, an act I had done countless times over the years. It was an arrowhead and I held it in my gloved hand, thinking of the hunter who dropped it there so long ago. I was standing on Cherokee hunting ground, after all.

You can spend ten minutes researching, get the basic information about the place you live—all the technical information—write a concise paragraph, and still not know anything really about the land.

Go outside. Right now. Put this book down and step outside.

Find North, then circle through all the directions. East. South. West. Back to North.

Day or night or somewhere in between. Sun, clouds. Moon, stars.

Weather.

Who else is out there? Birds, insects, animals, people. Listen and consider what you are hearing and what it all means.

Wiggle your feet. Breathe in as deeply as you can.

Treat the land like a new lover. Learn what it is, what it likes, how it is threatened and who protects it.

"Land" isn't only soil. It is wind and water. It is history and legend.

Who was there before you were there, and who will come after you?

You may find that coming into a meaningful relationship with your landbase requires you to slow yourself down, to set aside the distractions of modern life and to come more fully into a healthy relationship with yourself.

We'll do some of that tricky work in the next chapter.

Appalachian Churn Song

Come, butter, come!
Come, butter, come!

Chapter Two

Book-Learning and Uncommon Sense

Wisdom and information can come from many sources. Two of the favorites in the Appalachians are using your common sense and the kind of learning you get from reading. Common sense doesn't seem too common out in the broad world, so we'll consider that it comes from experience and observation and can, in fact, be learned experientially. Reading comes to us now in all sorts of media though our Ancestors, if they were able to read, generally read printed materials, often only the Bible or the works of Shakespeare (which sound very similar if you are reading the King James version of the Good Book).

I encourage you to seek knowledge in all available places and see what you learn about yourself and the world around you. This will help you in life and in your practice of folk magic. We want to look now at some helpful ways of learning from the natural world and the first step is to actually spend good time there. Ready?

We have seen reports of children who don't know where food comes from, that hamburgers are cows and catsup is made of tomatoes. As a culture, we

Americans are generally deficient in our connection with the environment. Many of you who are reading this book and doing these old practices are the exception to this generalization and I am grateful for that. But for those of you looking for ways of achieving and maintaining a more thorough engagement with the world around you, there are some helpful ways to be more connected to the land that holds you up. There are plenty of layers but I will break it down into a trio of key things—observation, kinship and book-learning.

Observation is just that: standing still and looking around you. It sounds terribly simple and it is, but many of us have lost the knack for stillness in the hurly-burly of our daily lives. On your way to the car (or the bus stop or the metro station) in the morning, give yourself an extra three minutes to look at the sky, observe the plants and critters, listen for birdsong and other sounds, smell the wind.

That's step one and it is harder to do than you might think. Like having a regular spiritual practice, making time in your schedule to engage with the natural world feels like a burden, one more thing on your already lengthy to-do list. It doesn't seem important.

It doesn't seem important until you do it.

I promise you that your world will expand, your life will have more meaning, and you'll be a better person for it. That may be a slight exaggeration but not by much. Seeing your smallness and youth compared to the mountains or the sea or a strong oak is a tonic for the little things that we let ourselves get pulled into. Taking a dose of this tonic every few days will do you a power of good, as the old folks say.

It is only the first step but it's a good one. With any luck, it will lead you to reading signs about impending weather changes and a desire to communicate with crows. Shoot, it may even have you trying to remember which constellation is which and to recognize clouds the same way you could in the fourth grade.

You are coming into relationship with the land around you and relationships sometimes bloom into something we may call kinship. You find yourself standing by the car, trying to understand a squirrel when you notice the weeds near the driveway. As you did with the clouds and Orion's Belt, you look it up and discover it is mugwort.

That is a mighty fine thing to know because mugwort is a sovereign herb, prolific and helpful, and it grows wild in lots of places. So you carefully cut some of the leaves and the smell of it delights you. See what you did? From observation to something a little dearer, something like kinship. And you'll start pointing it out to other people and showing off what you know, as we humans are wont to do. Then you won't let the homeowners' association people rip it up, explaining earnestly about how useful it is. Pretty soon you'll be growing lavender in a pot on the patio and moving onto wild plantain and eating dandelions and such. You might even come to understand that squirrel.

Good for you.

Those plants that once were background weeds have value to you now and you will hold dear a thing of value. That is a perfectly good step to valuing the whole of the natural world, of which we are also a part, and encouraging others to do so by both example and word.

I am so insistent about this because our Ancestors, the people who practiced this folk magic, lived in intimate relationship with the world because they had to. Their survival, which is also our survival, depended on it. Your practice of these more-or-less traditional folkways will be richly informed by your knowledge of and engagement with the world around you.

Which leads up to the other important piece of book-learning. Read a history of your town, your county, your state, and your region. Talk to old people who have lived in that place for decades, or generations. Go to the local library and ask for recommendations on what you should read.

Every being that has ever been in this land that is now your land has left an energetic imprint that can, with skill and practice, be discerned by the savvy rootworker.

Word to the wise.

One of the beauties of Appalachian folk magic—of hillfolks' hoodoo, as I call it—is its simplicity and the way it utilizes available materials, making them tools of your intention.This is a set of skills that most anyone can learn. Certainly some people are naturally more gifted than others. I play the piano but I am not a concert pianist. I would suspect that some of you have a natural aptitude for this work and others of you will have to practice it a bit more. There is no standard for this—you will practice it, tweaking your efforts if need be, until you can accomplish what you choose to accomplish.

These folk magic techniques are not dependent on your spiritual system or religion. Many people choose to add prayers and offerings to the Divines as part of this practice but that isn't necessary. That being said, however, I have found again and again that a working relationship with the land spirits in your area will bring you ease in working that is quite helpful. I begin most workings with an offering to the spirits of the land—a sup of something and a bite to eat. There is more detailed information in Chapter Ten on working with the Unseen folks.

Children grow up with a belief in magic that is fueled by stories in books and movies and by an innate certainty that the world is more than it seems.

Psychologists probably know when and why this changes for each of us. Practicing these simple magics affords you a chance to return to this place of wonder, where mystery is an always-sweet puzzle, and there is adventure and delight. Curiosity is one of the oddments for our work-basket, something to be encouraged and strengthened, a key to a successful and helpful practice. But it does require patience, as any skill does that you want to hone.

I often say to my students that practice makes perfect and I encourage them to do simple magics all the time. One of my pet peeves is the reluctance to use these energetic practices, to save them for a rainy day or when all else fails. You will never get to a comfortable skill level without the confidence of having the work, well, work for you.

I ask them to find a spell that is comfortable for them—the Parking Spell, the Burn Charm, Magic Hands for Finding—and use them all the time. You can't use up more than your allotment and you can't use it all up. You aren't being selfish to call up a parking space and you won't be cheating someone out of a space by setting your intention and using magic to accomplish it.

I do a little workshop called Simple Practical Magic and I am always surprised by the people who say they are witches or magicians but who don't actually do any magic and certainly don't practice enough to be adept.

They may be spending too much time reading all the books available on the subject without trying anything out. In the mountains we'd say they had too much book-learning and not enough common sense.

Both are important for this work you are exploring and—I hope—practicing. Read good books on the subject for both technique and history. And get yourself some practical experience by trying some simple magics. We're going to call that Uncommon Sense because there aren't too many people who have it, as you may have discovered.

What are some simple magics you can try? Let's review the ones mentioned above—the Parking Spell, the Burn Charm and Magic Hands. The intention of the Parking Spell is pretty clear—to find a parking space. There are so many little charms for this and I love them all. You can intone "Hail Asphalta, full of grace! Please find me a parking space!" You can invoke the Goddess Squat and ask her to sit in an empty parking space until you arrive there. What I do is simpler and doesn't involve creating helpful Deities. As I am sitting behind the wheel and before I've put on my seat belt or started the car, I say to myself—I am going to the library and I need a place to park. Then I go to wherever I am going and have mostly been rewarded with a space, even in difficult cities during hard-to-park times.

The Burn Charm is another helpful bit of folk magic

that I have employed countless times. There are many variations of this, too, and I often compare notes with other Appalachian folk about the verse used in their patch of the mountains. The first one I learned was this: "Come three angels from the north, take both fire and frost!" It is spoken aloud three times with a circular gesture about the burnt area. Another one is "Come three angels from the North—take fire, leave frost!" Other versions employ "Father, Son and Holy Ghost." Whatever the verse, the gesture is generally a circular motion over the burn, accompanied by blowing gently across the burn to blow the fire out.

Magic Hands for Finding will take some practice. I have always been a "finder" and am often employed to locate misplaced objects. Since my practice grows more intentional as I get older, I've devised a protocol for finding things and have given it the silly name Magic Hands.

Begin by grounding and centering, breathing deeply into your belly and stilling yourself and your surroundings. Rub your hands together until they are pleasantly warm. Hold in your mind an image of the lost thing. Turn your hands palms out in front of you and walk slowly through the area where the thing was last seen, if you know. Let your memory and intuition work together, especially if you are the one who lost it. You may find your hands are tingling a bit. This technique is also useful when you can't decide what to pack for a trip or what to make for supper or which present your mother would like best.

(For those of you who are unfamiliar with the practice of grounding, I have added an Addendum with it at the end of this book. But please use whatever technique works best for you.)

As with any craft, becoming competent at magic and energy work requires you to pay attention to the techniques that make the workings successful. Grounding, for instance, works swiftly and best when it is practiced often—every day, in fact. Same with shielding. Same with everything. Keep working it, tweaking it, making it your own. Start with simple magics and work your way into the deeper practices. Finding your footing in these shifting worlds takes a commitment to the work. You will find that the amount of time you dedicate to honing your skillset has to be somewhat fluid as the demands of life take bites out of your availability. But once you've committed to regular practice, you will find that some things start to be easy, effortless. And that is a satisfying feeling, indeed.

KJV Bibliomancy

Mountain folks have been known to look for answers through bibliomancy. Using the King James Version/ KJV of the Bible or maybe a complete Shakespeare, you sit with the heavy book in your lap and you consider the question you need an answer to. Close your eyes. Open the book at random and point your finger. Now open your eyes and read the answer. It is a kind of Appalachian I Ching, I reckon.

Chapter Three

Liminal Time and the Acquisition and Uses of Energy

Space and time change constantly, sometimes in large and overt ways that are tended by the entire culture—think Mercury in Retrograde or New Year's Eve or the Super Bowl. But more often, the shifts are subtle and indirect—the sorts of changes that bring us a kind of knowing, or kenning, that is deeply imbedded in our human fabric. I suspect all of you are familiar with that bone-deep knowledge or you wouldn't be pursuing magic to begin with.

In modern Paganism, we talk about two significant "hinges" in the Wheel of the Year—Beltane and Samhain—but the Wheel is broken into the familiar eight holy days, too. Solstices and equinoxes and four cross-quarters that are the subtle but significant shifts in the agricultural year. Time to plant, time to tend, time to harvest, and time to rest. Exquisite in its simplicity. As humans, we'd do well to follow those times more closely and to join in the natural world in its rising and its falling seasons.

On New Year's Eve shows, we watch the year

magically springing forth across every time zone, one by one, as the great Earth spins. This is a large hinge in our cultural year and is anticipated and celebrated as a time of both new beginnings and of the backward gazing so beloved of our species. And different cultures celebrate the ending/beginning at different times, so we can end and begin at Lunar New Year and Jewish New Year and Pagan New Year, et cetera.

In this chapter, we're going to explore liminality and how it fits into our practice of Appalachian folk magic. We will look at ways to harvest free energy for our work and will learn tricks to avoid using up your personal energy and draining your resources.

The concept of liminality comes down to us from the field of anthropology and the word itself comes from the Latin word that means "threshold." Isn't that interesting? Neither out nor in, like a willful cat. Not in one place or the other. It puts me in mind of hedges, too: those places between fields or between a field and a road. So many wild things flourish there, in the spaces in between. In a liminal place, on a threshold, we are not subject to the rules of either place and become free agents, in a sense. For our magical purposes, this is a fine place to stand—a place where anything might be possible.

I'd like you to consider what sorts of energy are waving through to be used or at least contemplated when the culture steps through one of these liminal places. We'll refer to that as "cultural energy." Focus on the New Year's hinge and think about the raising of energy through dance, music, expectation, and lust. As a person who is looking to affect change in the world, learning to sense that energy and harness it for the work you propose to do is a good technique to learn. Just as one can start fresh in the morning at the start of a new day, there's potential in an entire culture starting fresh at exactly the same time, whether intentionally or not.

In Addendum One at the end of this book, you'll find detailed instructions about relaxation, grounding and centering that I outlined in *Staubs and Ditchwater*. The shorthand for it is relax/ground/center/focus, which is often followed by a quick "shields up!" This is a helpful protocol for accessing earth energies and it works equally well for these cultural energies we're considering. Instead of pulling the energy up through your feet, however, adjust the technique to pull the energy in through your open hands, center it, set your intention and release it through the method that works best for you.

I suggest you practice these protocols as often as you can in preparation for deep energy work. It is best if you are able to get swiftly to this working state. I can't stress enough how important it is to do this quickly and begin working. When it seems to take more effort to prepare to do the work than it does to actually do it, you will be discouraged from making magic and that will be too bad. It is my personal belief that we need more magic, not less. We tend to save this as the last resort and your world and life will be simpler, tidier and less stressful when you have some agency over what happens to you and what you do with it. It is one of the first principals of folk magic—economy.

When you can easily access these stores of energy, you will avoid one of the pitfalls of working magic and one that is seldom spoken of. You will be using your techniques to access enormous energies and that means you don't have to use your own. You are a clean and strong vessel and the energy that is, for lack of a better phrase, your personal life force remains mostly untouched and continues to afford you good health and positive forward focus.

Just as a threshold is below our feet, above us is the lintel, the arching vault of the sky and all it contains. These energies are solar and lunar, comet and star. Using our same technique, open up the top of your head and pull the energy into your center, set your intention, and release it.

Appalachian people have used Moon signs to determine the timing for much of their farming lives and the power of the Moon is the one used most often in my circle of practitioners. The habit of observation that served you so well in the previous chapter will inform you about the phases of the Moon day by day. From Dark to New to Full and back again, the Moon is a drawing force as well as a filling one. Think for a moment about the tides, the ebb and flow, and imagine living in communion with those phases. Instead, many people focus on two phases—New and Full—and lose the fullness of living in synch with our little sister as she moves in her ways orbiting the Earth.

Many of us were taught to use the energy of the Full Moon, to prepare important workings for that time of Lunar power. I did that for years and years and then I met a Native woman from San Juan Capistrano. She explained that the women of her tribe had a tradition of not struggling at the time of the full Moon but would use that time to recharge their depleted energies. I tried it a few months later and found it to be a sweet time to rest, reflect and recharge, and I've done that ever since. Give it a try on the next full Moon—reserve some time out of your day (or better, your night) to absorb as much of that cool white energy as your little soul will hold.

Not all of us are gardeners or farmers, of course, but we can take the basic ideas that govern the agricultural year and expand on them for our best use. Think about planting time for a minute and imagine yourself deciding what goals you have set for yourself. Use the energy of the planting season to germinate ideas, to make changes in your personal or professional life.

Things that have been planted fare best when they are tended and taken care of in the long summer days. Rows of corn have to be cleared of weeds, mulched, watered and the weak seedlings removed to give the strong ones more room to grow and more nourishment from the soil. We all have things in life that require more tending than others, whether it is refreshing old skills in a foreign language or distancing ourselves from the people in our lives that are disruptive. Pruning away bad habits falls in with tending. Think about the common root of both tending and tender—how does our conscientious attention bring us to a place of deeper and more genuine connection with the world around us, the world of which we are a part?

Harvest time brings to mind pumpkins, baskets of apples, shocks of golden corn. During the fall harvesting season, turn your thoughts to reaping what you've planted in the spring and early summer. This keeps you in touch with those earlier intentions.

The final section of the agricultural year is winter: cold, still, the garden put to bed, the soil resting. Even though the dominant culture busies itself into a frenzy for the midwinter holidays, winter in nature's mode is a time of rest and renewal.

There is our Earth crucible—a time to plant, to

tend, to harvest and to rest rooted in the cycle of the seasons. There are so many hinges and energy points from which we can benefit and which we can use to enrich our work. Birthdays, various anniversaries, important national or regional events (for good or ill) are all sources of energetic renewal.

So many beautiful English words are associated with the transitioning place. Dawn, dusk, hedge, gloaming, verge. Old words and older concepts of times that are neither the one thing nor the other but a bit of both. A place between and beyond. I am a firm believer in demolishing binaries since most things are not one thing or another but a complex weaving that is a bit of both and a whole lot of something we haven't quite kenned.

There is power in the coming-together places and you would be wise to pay attention to the vibrant edges where chaos, invention and magic are bubbling over, waiting for the person who is savvy enough to engage with them.

Be a blessing as you step over the threshold.

Take a few moments to consider a personal blessing charm that can be used as needed. It can be as simple as "bless this place/person" or a little rhyming couplet: As my feet step through the door, let my blessing go before. You will feel like a modern-day Lady Bountiful. Be stealthy and also graceful as you bless all the world around you.

Chapter Four

The Five Needs

As my ideas about the needs of my clients and community develop, I have distilled them into something I call The Five Needs.

It is also a commentary on the things that drive us, that motivate us, and without which we feel an emptiness. We always practice discernment in this sort of work and you will be called upon to discern what you (or family member or client) are missing and what is impeding your progress to the place you want to occupy in the world and in your own life. It is not about neediness but it sometimes does have a tinge of desperation about it. As we dig more deeply into the human psychology that is the basis of simple magics, we are going to find ways to help that are healing, active and restorative.

This kind of simplification helps us when we are searching for materials and wondering how we can possibly master all the herbs, minerals, waters and the like in order to be both efficient and helpful. It can be overwhelming to think about the sorts of energy work that are possible and even the ones that are needed. Breaking it all down into manageable bits has been very helpful for me in my practice as I find ways to keep my work as direct and effective as possible.

The Five Needs:

- Protection
- Resources (including money, luck and love)
- Justice
- Healing
- Clarity (through divination and intuition)

These may seem self-explanatory but I'll give you a brief rundown of each one and what I put in each of the pigeonholes.

Protection: Energetic protection at a time when you or someone who comes to you for help is feeling particularly vulnerable or even "under attack." (I put that in quotation marks because I find that most people who think they are under attack from outside forces are simply in an emotional and intellectually vulnerable place and are actually shooting themselves in the foot, as it were.) This is about setting wards—even at a distance—and about shielding. We will also discuss talismans and sachets for general protective work.

Resources: We all know someone who needs a better job or who seems ridden by ill luck and can't seem to make a turn-around. Sometimes it's us.

Justice: We will discuss this at length because this section contains banework and hexing. Justice may be as simple as being treated fairly at work, giving energetic support in legal matters, or standing with a client during a nasty divorce.

Healing: I'm sure this is self-explanatory but I want to warn all of us that our healing capacity will have some limits, no matter how much we desire to do the work or how much the work is needed. Sometimes it is up to us to redefine what healing means and sometimes it is not our job to do.

Clarity: We carry within us so many strong resources and sometimes what we need to be able to do, or to help others to do, is to see a situation clearly and practice some non-attachment. Then we know what needs to be done. But often we are hampered by the cloudy murk of our emotions in a given situation and our histories with particular groups or people. We use some divinatory and meditative techniques to cut through the fog and see clearly.

Let's review the first of our Needs and line up some workings, banes and charms to go with each one.

Protection

This can be as simple as sending your friend home with a blessing of protection after Movie Night at your place or as complicated as a plea from someone to shield them until they are strong enough to do it for themselves. Think of three examples of protection that you've used for either yourself or another. Bestowing protection is something you can learn to do all the time. As you put on your seat belt (an obvious protective measure), go ahead and put protective shields around the whole car. When you rise in the morning, pull energetic shields around you as you prepare to face your day. Leave your hand on the doorway as you enter a friend's apartment and think to yourself—protect this home and all who enter here. It is quite the opposite of the banes that can sometimes be employed to stop a flow of energetic crap—you are leaving trails of blessings and protection everywhere you go. It is remarkably empowering and tends to put you in a very good mood.

Protocols include anointing, raising shields, setting wards and long-distance protection. Let's review each of them.

Anointing/Dressing. After grounding yourself, apply a drop of oil to the forehead, hands, feet, top of head (or wherever feels appropriate), as a token of protection.

Raising Shields. These are personal protections and should be strong and applied swiftly. You can also shield someone else.

Setting Wards. These are protective walls around a building or area.

Long-Distance Protection. Occasionally someone will need your energetic protection. She may be physically ill or stressed-out or otherwise debilitated.

You can do distance protection fairly easily by using the Silver Cord method.

I'll talk more about the Silver Cord a little later. It comes out of the Irish tradition and is sweet.

Resources

Resources are about acquisition of needful things and usually begin with Maslow's hierarchy (though I prefer to see that as a circle, myself). Without shelter, water, food, rest, et cetera, it is difficult to think in more esoteric terms. But once those are managed—job, home—it is time to think about a mate or spouse, about a kind of work that is fulfilling and important, about dealing with beings that have no physical place in our world.

Luck, love, money, good health/healing (though I will write more about that as another Need), reliable transportation, like-minded community—you can fill in with other resources you are lacking yourself or have helped others to acquire. And there are simple workings that can be used, using easy-to-get and wholesome materials, to bring energy and intention to bear on these needs.

It is important to always remember that these materials are simply tools, ways of focusing and directing your will and the energies around you in the planet and the sky. When you have come at last to the place where you can ground and begin working simply by focusing your considerable will and tapping into your energy sources, then you will be both efficient and effective. That is what we all strive for in this work. Getting the job done with a minimum of effort and a maximum of ability.

Justice

Justice is a tricky beast. We all have a good idea of what's fair in the world, based on our experience and discernment. We may have a general idea of the legalities under which we live in our county, state and nation. Some of you may have a more esoteric notion, or even a Divinity, that is a Platonic ideal of Justice. When we are talking about folk magic, we are generally dealing with two things when it comes to issues of justice—someone who needs your help to win a court case and someone who has little or no agency in their life and wants to gain justice through hexing. Both issues will involve your sharp discernment, your listening skills, and some very practical techniques and materials.

Let's take the first one first. I'm taking these scenarios out of my practice and will tell you what I did for each.

Scenario: A woman is going to court because her tenant pushed and slapped her during a dispute. The police were called and a report filed. I wasn't asked to delve into the larger and more complex issue of how difficult it is to eject a renter even if they smack you around. I was asked to be present with her in court, as a material witness to her stress level. But you may be asked to stand with a client as a kind of security blanket and you can decide if that's a good use of your time. What you are doing is acting as the client's surrogate and grounding both yourself and her.

More likely, though, you will be asked to supply some juice for the court case. This is standard operating procedure in most folk magics and you can buy Law Be Gone and Swift Justice and Friendly Judge candles in botanicas and dusty grocery stores.

There are oils that can be concocted—most come out of the Afro-Caribbean traditions.

In Appalachian culture, we will do almost anything to avoid "lawing" someone, including issuing our own rough justice. But the grannies know that some dirty dishwater is terribly effective, too. Dishwater is domestic in the extreme, but also elemental: earth, water, fire if you had hot peppers that day. You steep a strip of cloth (a rag) in the dishwater overnight and the next day you tie it onto a bush or tree off your property and preferably at a crossroad. As you tie the nasty sopping thing on to the branch (I always use three knots) you say something like—I am airing this out for (name). Let all come clean and (name) be free. You can also be a little trickier and do the same thing while changing that last sentence. Let all come clean and justice be swift. That way, if your client has lied to you, you don't end up helping a crook. You let the wheels of justice turn in the direction of rightness and you've only given it a little push.

You can also train a client to do a glamour so that they appear in the courtroom in such a way that they are seen to be trustworthy and honest. You can also undertake to do the work yourself and employ a binding spell on the appropriate target. The second option is much more ethically challenging and you must come up with your own rationale as to whether you engage in cursing/hexing. I refer to it as a category that I name "Banes." I will give you a more thorough rundown on the use of banes and whether or not those practices are for you. Many folks have such a deep-seated prejudice against this kind of work and much of that comes from the culture, from an upbringing in a very strict religious tradition or because their magical training is of the soft-Wiccan variety—all of which labor under the strictures of doing no harm. Older traditional witchcraft systems worldwide use banes as a form of healing, oddly enough, and that's where my ease in these workings comes from. There is a truism—if you can't hex, you can't heal. It is the sense that poor people/peasants/the disenfranchised don't have much hope in a system that is rigged against them, in which money and power speak more loudly than justice and fair play. We all know examples of this and have probably experienced it ourselves—the boss that blames you for their mistake, the speed trap where you really were going within the speed limit, the ex who demands visitation time with a child they have emotionally or physically harmed.

It is an extreme kind of healing, to be sure, like amputation or chemotherapy. But it is sometimes necessary and often asked for. There are so many techniques for banes that I have to know it is a very popular form of magic. As I wrote above, I want to go more thoroughly into these. I've developed a system for it. We will look at this in more depth in Chapter Ten.

Healing

Healing. Bringing into wholeness. Alleviating pain. Bringing ease to the dis-eased. This is a biggie. It encompasses so many things and yet, I suspect you all have a grasp of what it means to be a healer. You have all taken this on for precisely that reason—to make the world whole.

I'll skip the "what is healing" except to say that sometimes helping someone become whole means that you are holding space for that person to make a transition out of illness through the doorway of death. Sometimes we are helping folks come to terms with their disability in a way that still gives them power and agency in their own world. Sometimes it is holding space or standing allied with a broken healer who is doing their own work—then you are almost like those old-time magician's assistants—distracting the well-wishers and family while the patient does the necessary healing. This healing thing is mind, body, spirit, Universe, zeitgeist.

I use a variety of herbs and some minerals for sachets for the patient. Are we all okay with referring to the one who needs healing as a patient? Dried leaves of witch hazel, poke, vervain, wild mint, et cetera, and stuffed into a little pouch or folded up in brown paper to carry in a pocket. I dress candles and either burn them on my own altar or give them to the patients (if they are local). I buy plain white candles; my favorites are the ones used for Jewish Shabbats. They are about the size of emergency candles and come in a box of 72. You can usually find them in a well-stocked grocery store.

I dress them with my favorite healing oil, which is a cedar essential oil base, with citrus notes (lemon or tangerine).

This work sometimes (okay, mostly) requires the assent of the patient and will be more effective if the one who is ill enters into the spirit of the healing. It is difficult to do healing for someone who doesn't believe this can work or is psychologically or emotionally benefitting from being sick. We've all met people like that—folks who are tied to their sickness and can use it as a way to retreat into safety or to gain attention that is otherwise lacking. So the eager assent of the patient and both of you knowing that you are there in love and friendship to do what you can is really important.

The approach we are taking to all of these is a homeopathic one and one that involves our own access to energy as well as our intention and will.

Western medicine has given us a blue million pharmaceuticals for all of the things mentioned—and these products work with varying degrees of success.

Truth be told, when it comes to some of the ailments that plague modern culture (depression, anxiety, and sleeplessness), only depression would have been recognized in the old days in the mountains. Women were often "blue" or "down"— and who could blame them, given the hard life of subsistence farming on thin soil and the often patchy ability to control your reproductive life. Men generally self-medicated with homemade alcohol, unless their religion banned its use and, even then, it was often disguised as patent medicines. Whiskey of varying qualities was often kept as a remedy for things like snakebite. And Lydia Pinkham had a range of medicines for the housewife that was available through traveling salesmen or at the general store. These remedies contained alcohol, cocaine, and laudanum—all sorts of pain-killing ingredients.

But anxiety would have been a real part of mountain life. There was always something to be anxious about—fire, weather, sickness. They would have tried to pray or work it away and would not have thought of it as an ailment. Likewise, sleeplessness is rare when your day is long and filled with manual labor.

These three diseases are rampant in modern society, however, and that's where we, as Appalachian-style magic workers, live. Let's consider what we already know and see what might be used effectively for all of the above.

Depression: I approach this energetically, magically. I first ask clients to learn and then practice shielding and wards. I ask them (or help them) to set up an energy trap. If they are spiritual people, I suggest prayer and/or meditation. If they are meat-eaters, I suggest beef—as rare as they can stand it, about three times per week. I will sometimes suggest vigorous exercise, if they are in a state where they can do that. (Often people suffering with depression simply can't do anything.) Good herbs to have nearby for depression are lavender and rosemary. I stress that protecting themselves from outside influences (shields and energy trap) can give them a breathing space which in turn can help with targeting the cause (if there is a cause) and addressing that. Depression requires constant monitoring, support, and tough love. It is really, really hard to treat in this way but it is possible.

Anxiety: I believe anxiety is present when the client has a sharply honed flight-or-fight reflex, and that those responses are nearly almost the wrong choices in our modern world. I do the usual—move them to herbal teas and tisanes and away from caffeine. Long walks, observing nature, in the company of calm and confident people. There's a small working that seems to be effective. Place a bowl in the middle of a table and surround it with small rocks or buttons or dried beans. When anxiety flows through you at home or work, stop, breathe through it, try to recognize what has triggered you, and drop a rock into the bowl, letting the Universe/ bowl hold that worry for you. Good herbs for anxiety are Joe Pye weed and kudzu blossom.

Sleeplessness: My go-to for sleep-related things, including dreams, is mugwort. I make little sachets of the dried herb that can be tucked under the pillow and have even suggested a client cut a bunch of fresh mugwort and put it in the pillowcase, under the pillow. The smell seems to stimulate and regulate dreams, and several clients have reported being able to sleep through the night with regular use. I also recommend creating and following a nighttime routine.

Clarity

The last Need to address is Clarity. Clarity means two things—your clarity on the issue for a client, and helping clients find their own clarity in a given situation.

Clarity for your client:

You will have people come to you who are confused about their lives, incapable of moving forward, not sure what to do next. Most people already know what they should do but they may need your listening ear and open heart to help them find the courage to reach out and do what they know should be done. Listening is a good starting place—and asking leading questions. Suggest that they write down their dreams for seven days and see what they're getting from the ether. Do a reading in a system you do well—cards, pendulum, runes, scrying—and advise your client based on that.

For your own clarity:

I often talk about discernment and what I mean by that is observation, combined with intuition and common sense. Discernment is an important part of you, as a rootworker, having clarity about a situation. Listening, observing, pondering, and then action. Setting aside any emotion that is not love and opening your heart, your mind, and your spirit, and sensing what is wrong, what is needed. It can be so simple—like magic! But when you are clouded up, it is unnecessarily difficult. Remember your own practice: relax, ground, center, focus, work. Then listen to your intuition and trust your gut. It will always serve you to remember these basics of the practice. It will not help you to feel that the situation is a dire emergency and act without the benefit of that practice. You may save yourself a few minutes but you won't be at your peak and you won't be doing your best work.

Seeing Clear

Often we are fogged up with too much information and too many worries. If you feel like you can't see the forest for the trees, try this little mica spell. Get a piece of mica at least as big as a silver dollar. Set it on a piece of dark cloth or paper. Peer at it, noticing the flakes, the edges, and the shine. With the middle finger of your dominant hand, tap the middle of the mica. Close your eyes as you tap and tap slowly. Nice deep breaths now and say to yourself—what am I not seeing? All this shiny, what is it blinding me to? What do I know—what do I ken—that is just at the corner of my mind but I can't quite grasp? You may be surprised at all the things that pour into the front of your mind. Might be good to have a pen and some paper handy.

Chapter Five

Your Work-Basket—Tools, Containers, and Materials

Since writing the first book, my personal practice has grown and changed, because folk magic practices are living traditions based in the tangled mess that is any given culture. There's a light treatment of tools and materials in that book, but I have new ones to share and don't want to repeat that information here. There is a list of useful tools in the Appendix, if you are wondering what else could come in handy for this work.

In Chapter One, we got familiar with the concept of a work-basket and I hope you have come up with a suitable storage case for your wares. This chapter is focused on what goes into that work-basket and what you do with these bits and bobs.

It may be that you won't be able to fit all these things in your little work-basket so I encourage you to have a shelf or a couple of boxes to hold the paraphernalia you use occasionally but not all the time. Workings with herbs, minerals and waters can lead you to collect a fair number of helpful things. Surely you may do almost anything with a sharp knife and a stout wooden bowl but it won't stop there, if you're like me.

Here are a few of my favorite things, as the song says.

Tools

I am still using a big, old mortar and pestle that was given to me by my friend, Mary. It had belonged to her mother who used it for herbs and spices, but Mary didn't have much use for it so she passed it on to me when her mother died. It doesn't travel with me because it is big—seven inches tall with a nine-inch pestle, and it weighs seven pounds. It is handmade of glazed stoneware. I have a smaller one for grinding things that should not be ingested but sometimes I break those herbs down between two flat rocks out in the yard.

Some kind of grinding apparatus is handy so I advise my students to get one. They are readily available in kitchen stores and thrift stores.

As with any sort of tool, you may find your first fumbling efforts to be disheartening but don't despair. Practice does make perfect, or at least it makes you skilled with that tool. You can practice grinding things that like a heavy hand. A good choice for grinding practice is red clay mud harvested wet and allowed to air dry. It takes a patient hand to grind that into fine redding and many people find that the work of grinding gives them the chance to let their minds wander, as they did when they were children. We get some surprising wisdom about the world and ourselves when we daydream while working. And you can't hurt yourself, the mortar, or what you're grinding when you have gone woolgathering.

I have a collection of good knives and it is up to you to decide what kind of knife—size, shape of blade and weight—works best in your hand. You may need several styles for different applications. I have a Swiss Army knife, an oyster-shucking blade, and an Old Hickory paring knife with a four-inch blade, which belonged to my grandmother. I keep a good set of knives in my kitchen, of course, and will draft one of those into service if need be. Thrift shops are a good place to look for these, too.

While we're on the subject of blades, let me put in a good word for learning to sharpen yours. A dull blade is worse than useless, it's downright dangerous. It used to be there was always some old fella at the horse auction or the flea market who was set up to sharpen knives and you'd load up yours in a kitchen towel and gossip with the other folks as he carefully sharpened up your blades.

But if you don't have a flea market fella or an old dude at the hardware store to do it for you, it is easy to learn how. You can ask amongst your friends for someone to teach you—that would be best—or you can find some good videos online that walk you through the process. A straight blade is fairly easy to sharpen and you will be proud of yourself when you can do it with a steel or a stone. You may also need some steel wool, some oil (like Three-in-One) and rags. I sometimes use lambs' ears—that soft grey plant that is so invasive in the yard—to wipe the blade down after sharpening. Keep your tools sharp and your mind open in life and you'll probably do all right.

It's a superstition in the mountains that you never give a gift of a knife without getting money in return or else the relationship will be cut asunder. So I buy you a nice new knife for your birthday and you give me back a penny (though a shiny dime is better). Sometimes in sets of knives, the giver will go ahead and place some coins inside the velvet-lined box and the recipient will open it and hand the coins right back to the giver, without a word being said.

We'll go over harvesting and wildcrafting in the next chapter but a tool you'll need for that is a small pair of pruners, what I call secateurs. Get yourself a good pair at either the garden center or the hardware store and carry them with you when you're tending to or looking for herbs. It is easier on the plant to have a bit snipped away than for you to tear the branch and leave a jagged wound. It is also easier on your hands.

Speaking of your now-calloused and strong hands,

there will be times when you will need to wear gloves. Many gardeners prefer to work barehanded but I have regretted that choice on more than one occasion. Cutting spring nettles is a good example of the need for some hand protection. My daughter got me a very fine pair of leather rose gauntlets that protect my wrists and forearms, as well as my hands. My, don't I feel elegant wearing those pretty gloves.

Other tools you may find handy for busting things up is a rock pick and a hammer. Have you ever stood at the hardware store looking at all the kinds of hammers there are? It is astounding. Find one whose weight and length fit your body type and what you plan to use it for. If you're unsure, ask the hardware store person for advice. And for pete's sake, go to a hardware store, if there is one in your town. If you go to one of those "home improvement stores," the staff is going to be scant and will often have no idea how to help you. You will probably find a rock pick not too far away from the hammer section.

The little digging implement called a trowel is handy for smaller roots and stones and such. You have a couple of choices on this, depending on your budget and temperament. You can invest is a heavier one where the handle is a built-in part of the trowel and it will last a long time but it will be pricier. Or you can plan on getting a new one every year and spending less for it. I like my hands to get used to my tools so I prefer to use a tool for a good long time and I finally went with the first choice. But either one works.

You may find you need a small handsaw for a variety of things, from firewood to pruning. Handsaws take some tending to keep them sharp. Don't let them stay wet or sticky. Be diligent about cleaning them before you put them away and they will reward you with many years of loyal service.

Your brazier—or "brassiere" as someone in my high school Latin club pronounced it—can be anything from a little cast-iron cauldron to a fire pit to a bonfire. Smaller is more practical, of course, but a group of you sitting around a side yard fire pit and plotting your work and flinging it into the fire is very satisfying. A cast-iron pot, like a Dutch oven, works very well. Or you can go ahead and claim your witchiness and get yourself a cast-iron cauldron. Whatever sort of burning bowl you choose, I am trusting that you will be sensible about using it properly and will avoid having to use the Burn Spell in its many manifestations. And if you don't, you'd better harken back to our earlier encounter with that helpful little spell.

I've been saying for many years that I want to learn to make fire from scratch—to strike new fire—with a stone and steel. But I haven't taken the time to do that yet. It does sound like a powerful thing to be able to make fire and I believe I'd like the dramatic possibilities. I have some friends who spin fire and spit fire and that is a sight to see. I did a memorial service for a young man who had died suddenly and his good friend lit the fire at the beginning of the ceremony by spitting a stream of fire out of his mouth onto the dried wood. He made me look good, that fella.

My work-basket contains several bells and whistles, including the kind of cowbell that goes on a cow. I have a pennywhistle and a clay ocarina. There's my great-grandmother's old dinner bell and a tough little bell that looks like a Christmas tree that I use for tight spaces. I use them for calling up spirits and then for soothing them. And whistles, including the kind of whistling you do when you pucker up your lips and blow, have been used since times past as a way to bring up the wind or whistle up some good luck.

Containers

By now, you have a collection of canning jars and recycled mayonnaise jars that you can use for storing or tincturing. Some other containers you may find useful are baskets in all shapes and sizes. I like those old-fashioned half-bushel baskets from the farmers' market but I always have a blessed sufficiency of baskets on hand.

I use the colanders from my kitchen to carry all kinds

of herbs. There's a battered plastic one, a wire-mesh one, and a big stainless steel beauty that can hold gallons of berries.

I have yet to figure out the purpose of these purple and green Mason jars you see around stores. What can you can in a purple jar besides grape products or pickled beets, I wonder. Likewise, the green ones. Yes, indeed, pickles are beautiful in them, as well as green beans. But they don't do much for squash or chow-chow.

Materials

Dirts, dusts, waters and stones. I touched on the use of dirts, dusts and water in *Staubs* but I think these important materials deserve more time than I gave them. As a practitioner, you need more information about these traditionally used materials. And I have added information on stones as I have come to use them on a more regular basis.

As far as I can tell from my research, the bulk of the work with actual dirt and dust, ashes, sand, dry powder, et al., comes out of the Tsalagi tradition. (I'm trying to be intentional about using the word that the "Cherokee" use for self-identification but am conscious that some of them prefer "Cherokee" and some do not. As with most things, if I get to that stage in a relationship with a person who self-identifies as one or the other, I'll ask which they prefer. Seems easier than me trying to guess.) The uses of special waters, willow, thunder, snowmelt, et cetera, seem to come out of the British Isles—or so my preliminary research tells me.

Both sets of materials are used for purification, for setting intention, for getting your intention "out there" and for healing (including hexing). We'll start with dirts and dusts. First, a list with a definition—though most are self-explanatory—and then what I use them for.

Redding: Brick dust comes out of the African diaspora traditions. I dry red clay mud and grind it up in my trusty mortar and pestle. Either way red dirt is usually referred to as redding.

Daubers' Nests: You see these throughout the summer. They are mud-constructed tubes that are usually on the sides of buildings and usually high up.

Sand: Dry, granular dirt.

Dried Excrement: You have much to choose from— horse, cat, human. Always wash your hands after using this particular material.

Wood Ash: What you rake out of the fireplace or wood stove. It is mostly used for soap making but it is handy for other things, too.

I am very fond of redding, which is not traditional to Appalachian folk magic but is borried from the Afro-Caribbean practice. I make travel talismans from it, I love to gather and grind it up in the little mortar and pestle. My friend, Ebiaz, concocted a wonderful device for pouring redding that consists of a mid-sized Mason jar with a funnel attached to the top to make a spout. It is sealed onto the top of the jar with the canning ring that comes with the jar. Transportable and easy to run a nice bead when you need it. Redding is used for protection. It is placed on the major entrances and egresses in a house or other building by running a bead of it just at the doorjamb.

Daubers' nests are used primarily in healing ceremonies and workings. The wasp is a tough little critter and very determined. The ground up dauber dust can go in a pouch or a little sachet to give you some extra energy and to remind you that you take your home with you wherever you go. It is particularly good in a talisman for good sexual health for men. I suppose because the dauber tubes have a kind of phallic shape.

Sand is most often used in purification, especially in a house or room where someone is or has been sick. You scatter the sand on the floor and the window ledges, leave it a bit and then sweep it up. Then you take it to the edge of the property and you let the sand carry the disease away. Holding it in your open palm, you blow it off and away.

Poop can be used for lots of things. Imagine the animal it comes from. Do you want the strength of a bear? The swiftness of a deer? The fertility of a

bunny? You can set a spell over the poop—bring me the swiftness of a deer! In this job interview, let me be clever as a fox—that sort of thing. Then bury it in the yard, return it to the Earth for composting. You might choose to wear some rubber gloves for working with this material.

Wood ash holds the essence of the tree from which it comes and also holds the essence of the fire that burned it. A hearth fire from good dry oak. A summer bonfire with your friends where you burn the pruned apple boughs. Think about the situation as well as the materials and use them for healing, to bring resources, etc. Apple ash is good for prosperity workings. Oak is a strong tonic for folks with chronic illness. The ash can be kept in a sachet if you are drawing to you or blown away from the palm as outlined above if you want to rid yourself of an influence.

Likewise, I'll list out the waters and then we'll work through them for further information about usage.

Waters:
- alcohol
- willow water
- stump water
- snowmelt
- thunder and lightning water
- ditchwater
- dishwater

Alcohol means drinking alcohol. My preference is corn liquor: culturally speaking, it is the most appropriate. But I also use Irish whiskey, wine, and beer. Alcohol is a wonderful offering to activate your unseen companions. Different spirit beings prefer different things. You can find out through trial and error. My land folk—the ones I call the Cousins—they like corn liquor and also beer. The apple trees like mulled wine.

Willow water is best when it is the stump water from an old willow tree. But that is very hard to come by so I make willow water by soaking the fresh new branches of willow in the early spring in spring water or purified water. *Nota bene*: the best waters to use for workings are fresh spring water or fresh well water. Second best is putting both those waters into a milk jug and holding them on your workbench. Willow water is mostly used in healing. Laying a cooling cloth on the forehead soaked in cool but not cold willow water can ease a headache. In the old days, it was ingested for digestive needs but I don't recommend that unless you trust the rain where you are and also trust the stump that gathers it in. Otherwise, leave the water to work its magic through the outside of the body.

Stump water is used for setting protective wards around a property. It is used for anointing people and animals when they are going through an ordeal of some kind—sitting for the SAT, having surgery, etc. Just like perfume, it goes on the pulse points. Stump water is rainwater that has gathered in a stump. It must be gathered as fresh as possible or it gets greened up with algae. It has also been used traditionally for healing.

When there's a big snow, go out and gather up some and let it melt in your Mason jar. Use it to cool things down and help you regain focus. Too heated up by a situation to react effectively? That's a place for snowmelt. Feeling like a teeny-bopper over a totally inappropriate person? Dab some snowmelt on.

I love the idea of thunder and lightning water, don't you? It is water that is gathered in a rainstorm in which there is thunder and lightning. To be most effective, you must brave the storm and gather the rain. It's not so strong if you dash out of the house with a washbasin and leave it under the downspout. And it is even less effective if you simply dip some of last night's storm water out of your rain barrels. You need to make a commitment for thunder and lightning water. It is used to call storms, to bring rain to parched gardens, to give you the guts to do what needs to be done. It gives you the courage to stand up to bullies and bring the wrath of the sky with you. Dab it on, as always. Don't ingest.

Ditchwater is rain that is standing in a muddy place,

like a ditch. There aren't so many earthen ditches as there were when people lived on dirt roads, but they are still around, if you keep your eyes open. Ditchwater is very watery mud—or maybe very muddy water. It usually has critters in it—microscopic and otherwise. It is stagnant water but filled with life. Only gather as much as you need for a working and leave the rest to be the wonderful matrix of goo that it is. I use ditchwater to set things in motion, to bring small ideas to fruition. Here's an example I'm doing right now. I got a mid-size Mason jar and scooped up some ditchwater and put it on my workbench. Every day I add a little more water to it, to lighten it up and make it "grow." It's for a future project that I'm researching.

Dishwater is that disgusting stuff that's left after you've washed the dishes. It's clammy and greasy and has bits of food in it. Grey water is what we call it in permaculture land. It isn't really dirty, especially if you're careful about the detergent you use, but it is unsavory. Dishwater is used as it was used in the first place—to get rid of something. Set the intention onto a rag of some sort. You can write it on there or say words over the rag as you set your intention. Stop smoking, stop eating chocolate cake every day, stop obsessing about (fill in the blank). You get the idea. Then soak the rag in the dishwater and then bury it outside, off your property. Best to do so on a dark Moon. In fact, any kind of banishing or shedding or ridding work is best done on a dark Moon.

We're going to finish up with staubs. Staubs come out of the rich tradition that includes wands, staves, quarterstaves, walking sticks, brooms, crutches, canes—any piece of good wood that supports you in your life and work. Sometimes in the summer I think of a Popsicle stick as a little staub. A maypole is a mighty big staub, but it comes with a big intention, too.

A staub is a little longer than a piece of stovewood but about as thick. Let's say two inches in diameter and about fifteen inches long. A tomato stake will do in a pinch. You use a staub to mark territory. It can set up the bounds of your yard and can be used to mark out where new fencing will go. For our purposes, you can use a staub to set wards of protection around your property. You can use a single staub as a place to set out offerings for your Ancestors or land spirits. You can attach a war bottle to it and set it swinging.

It is a marker, a sign both outward and inward of setting up your intention. You can set one up in celebration after you've finished that big job. You can set one up in memoriam when someone you love has died. You can set a staub to draw sickness from someone who is ailing.

As with everything, you may choose to be intentional about the kind of wood for your staub. Oak for strength, willow for healing, apple for joy, pine for flexibility.

Stones: I am not one of those folks who knows the proper gem or crystal to use for a particular effect in a specific situation. I like rocks. I pick them up when I travel and I find them to be friendly as well as beautiful. For the record, this part of the world is incredibly mineral rich. When I was little, there was a rock shop in the little township we visited for groceries on Saturday mornings and it was always worth a visit. I now go to the periodontist in the same township and yesterday I was a little early for my appointment. With some glee, I noticed that a rock shop has opened in the building next door and they even have a sluice for the kids to look for gems. Perfect. There are several native minerals here that I use most often.

Mica: I use this in place of mirrors in workings that require them. It was mined in this area for decades and rumor had it there was an old mica mine on the mountain where I grew up. I was up there a lot but never found any scary mine entrance. I did find bunches of mica and was always warned by the grown-ups to be careful and not get it in my eyes because it would blind me.

If you are lucky, you can find a big hunk of it. It flakes off—you can use the sharp point of a knife to pry up the edge and release it from the larger clump in one smooth piece. It is used commercially as an insulator. And it is sometimes called isinglass. There is a song from the musical *Oklahoma,* "Surrey with the Fringe on Top," which references "with isinglass curtains you can roll right down." These thin sheets of mica were also used as peepholes in boilers and as the sides of lanterns because the mica could withstand a lot of heat.

I used it as a mirror in small energy traps but it is also useful anywhere you need something shiny. If you are doing a working to draw attention to someone's good (or bad) qualities, mica is a perfect addition. It is handy when working with land spirits as they like sparkly things.

It comes in many colors, as I learned at the Colburn Earth Science Museum, but the most readily available is silvery, like fish scales.

Clay: You all know what I do with red clay mud but there are all kinds of clays that are available in this part of the mountains. In fact, there is so much that within walking distance from my house, and on the banks of the French Broad, there is a company that sells beautiful ceramic clays—porcelain and stoneware and earthenware.

Think about the properties of clay for a moment. Damp, cool, malleable. And then it dries firm. It is glazed and glazed again. It goes into the fire and all imperfection is burned away—or else it explodes in the kiln, shattered to rubble. When the fire is gone and the kiln and pottery have cooled, it emerges completely altered and completely perfect.

Garnetstone: When I think about my childhood, my cousin Dena and I were always up to mischief of some sort. We once lugged a very heavy piece of rock off the mountain because we thought it had cave painting on it. The grown-ups assured us it was just veins of other rock with some naturally occurring rust. I wish I still had that rock, to be honest. We also found smaller rocks with garnets in them and would spend happy hours with a hammer and a tobacco pouch busting out the rubies in the rock.

The word garnet has the same Latin root as pomegranate, and that is helpful in determining how to use these pretty stones. It is also used commercially as an abrasive. You have a stone (seed) that is the color of blood and can be used to rub away unwanted bumps and to smooth surfaces.

Gravel: We all know what gravel is, I reckon. Little rocks that came from big rocks. The stuff in the driveway and on the garden paths. What we don't often consider are the mines where gravel and other stone are cut from the mountains. If you travel up Highway 221, north from Interstate 40, you will see plenty of stone companies, sales and extraction.

You can buy a column of flat stone wrapped in wire to use in your hardscaping endeavors or to face your building. You can have gravel delivered for your paths and it is graded by size—from little peas to silver dollar-sized. You buy it by the pound, by the ton, if it is a big project.

Here is what that humble gravel is, dear reader—it is the heart of ancient mountains.

I'll leave you with that thought for a minute.

You can walk out to where your car is parked and pick up a fistful of mountain heart. What kind of power and wisdom do you reckon is in your little hand right now?

Look at that handful closely and notice the variety of stones. Look at the dull colors and peer at the striations within the main rock. Feel the weight in your hands. Now put that bit of gravel in a bowl and put some water on it and watch the transformation of the colors.

River Rock: I am lustful about river rock. I blame it on this campsite we used to visit when I was a kid. We had so much fun there and I'd always come home with those soft-looking rounded stones. They usually lined flowerbeds in the front yard or I stacked them up into cairns.

I still carry within me that lust for river stone. I still collect it whenever I can and it lies about our yard, just as it did in the yard out in west Buncombe. The bed that holds the flowering tobacco has perfectly white ones and the bed that holds the new asparagus plants has river rock that is honey-colored.

Stone and water, river and rock: each working on the other, giving the water her voice, smoothing the rough from the rock. Magically, river rock is used for realizing long-term goals, for slow manifestation. Because it is heavy, a charm can be written on paper and tied to a river stone. Left on your altar or your workbench for the appropriate amount of time to juice up the working, then you walk with it to the river, speak your intention to it and to the spirits of the water. Then, with a final kiss for luck, lob it in.

Give Me Strength

We all go through times when we feel lower than a fishing worm. No get-up-and-go and no self-confidence. We feel small, used up, and vulnerable. We are in need of a little boost. Wait for a full Moon, if you can. Get some gravel from your driveway or the parking lot at the barbeque place. Take a chair outside and sit where you can see the Moon. (If it is raining, you can sit indoors by the window. If it's cloudy and you can't actually see the Moon, sit outside and know that it's there, even if you can't see it.) Sit with a deep bowl or cup in your lap, between your knees, and make sure the bowl is half full of water. Ground deeply and breathe your way to some quietness. As you look at the Moon, drop the gravel pieces (that shattered heart of the mountain) one by one into the water. Say to yourself something like—the heart of the mountain sustains me, my heart is stronger because of my kinship with the stone, the Earth and the Moon above me. Pull energy up through your feet as you drop those little stones in. When you are finished, leave the bowl outside under the Moon and use the heart of the mountain all month long to revive your own heart and your strength.

Chapter Six

Wildcrafting and Growing Your Own Granny Garden

We must go and gather
The seven herbs of fall.
Not wait for the washing nor
Anything at all.
We must go and pick them for
The healing of us all.
A summons from the Mother are
The seven herbs of fall.
O, the Ladies o!
They walk with their baskets
Swinging to and fro.
The seeds sift through and
Their clogs break up the grass and
The holy weeds flourish where e'er
The Ladies pass.

The Seven Herbs Seasonal Cycle

Since learning the beautiful "Seven Herbs of Spring" song from our Beloved Crone Antiga, I've been playing around with my favorite magical plants for each season.

I did fall first, then added the other two seasons. These are the ones I love—please take a look at them and note which ones are your favorites for each season. Many of them are available in more than one season—mugwort and parsley, for instance, are available in every season. For your consideration, the Seven Herbs Seasonal Cycle is attached near the end of this book, as an addendum.

When I was growing up in the wilds of west Buncombe county, my mother told stories of my great-grandmother, who lived in the same neighborhood where I live now. She and her husband had brought their family from a neighboring county in the waning years of the 19th century and had opened a little grocery store. I have a photo of her sitting on her back stoop, hands folded, squinting toward the camera.

One of the good stories was how Grandmaw would go out in the field across from the house with a dishpan and would pick all manner of weeds, then come inside and cook them up. They were delicious! I wanted to be able to do that, too—to know the yummy greens from the ones that would make you sick. It was only later that I realized she had to do a great many things to keep so many mouths fed, especially when her husband was often without steady work.

I am able to do that and you can do it, too, depending on where you live. Going out in the early spring to pick the first dandelions, violets, chickweed and nettles is a delight, pure and simple.

Wildcrafting is a modern buzzword for going out into your backyard or an unused, untended space and picking the weeds that grow there. Another popular word for it is foraging. Wildcrafting should be done with love and care. The ethical way to do it is to take only what you need, never take the entire plant (unless you are harvesting a root, then you need to make sure there are plenty more around before you take the essence and future life of that particular specimen), don't pick in places where it is illegal (like national parks), and never take an endangered species.

People choose to do wildcrafting when they want to be sure of the freshness and origins of the plant. Let's be honest about price, too. It is thriftier to pick your own than to buy from even a local shop or farmers' market.

You will need a good book with pictures of the plants that grow in your area that can be harvested, used for magical purposes or eaten. It is also helpful if there are people in your community who do plant walks and can show you what to pick and what to leave alone.

What follows are my Thirteen Good Herbs and True—the plants that I regularly harvest either from my yard or from overgrown fields that I know. And that's an important thing to consider, too, when you are wildcrafting. Spend some time with the land and see who else frequents it. That could be a beautiful stand of dandelions because it's where all the neighborhood dogs do their business, if you get my meaning. The greens may look pretty but it also may take you a lot of washing to feel like they're edible. However, if the dogs are doing the same to a likely patch of something that you don't intend to ingest, you may not care a fig. And if someone owns the land, it is always a kindness to ask permission before you stray onto that little piece of the great world.

Here they are, in order of appearance in the spring in the southern highlands:

Witch hazel, chickweed, dandelion, stinging nettles, mugwort, plantain, rabbit tobacco, mountain mint, elderberry, Queen Anne's Lace, poke, Gentleman's Walking Stick, 'sang.

I am mostly talking about the magical uses for these plants and only recommend you eating them if I have done so and if it is delicious. Many of these are used for healing various things in Appalachian folk medicine. I have noted that, but am also here to tell you that there are real doctors in this world who will also take good care of you. If you have a serious health issue—or think you might—leave the folk remedies to their historic place.

Witch-hazel (hamamelis virginiana)

Witch-hazel is a plant that blooms in the late winter and sets its leaves after that. The flowers have a sweet smell and I pluck some of those and bring them in for the cheery color and scent in the last weeks of true winter here. I use the leaves for magical purposes though you can get witch-hazel in alcohol commercially and it is a great astringent for the skin. Witch-hazel like that has been used in traditional Appalachian homes for decades as a way to ease a bruise, or pumpknot— the kind of wound from a striking blow that raises a knot under the skin. I dry the new leaves, after the plant has flowered, and I use them in sachets to bring myself or my client clarity and wisdom.

Chickweed (stellaria media, also called chickenwort)

I have been known to graze through young chickweed in the springtime, like a two-legged cow. It is so deliciously bright green after a grey winter and it is almost irresistible. It is good to eat out-of-hand, in a salad or as pesto. It smells of sweet corn silk and because of that smell, I use it aromatherapeutically, by pulling a swag of it and giving it a good sniff. Magically, I use it as an herb of renewal for projects, as well as my own spirit. It can be dried and put in a cotton bag or a sachet.

Dandelion (taraxacum officinale)

I don't need to tell you what dandelions look like, do I? They are the weeds everyone loves to hate and I can't figure out why. They are delicious cleaned and sautéed in olive oil. Their roots can be roasted and eaten, or made into a nourishing tea. They are cut-and-come-again plants. The more you harvest them, the more they produce. Young and tender leaves are the most flavorful but even the older leaves are good, if you don't mind a little bitterness. They are good in omelets, too. Dandelion is green and golden and white and the seeds are natural wish-bringers. What child doesn't know to wish on the fluffy seed-head and then blow all those seeds into the sky? I use it magically—in sachets or dollies—to aid in making dreams come true and to help clients find ways to know their heart's true desire.

Stinging Nettles (urtica family)

O, how I love nettles! I make nettle tea. In fact, there's a half gallon Mason jar in my fridge right now. It is a perfect spring tonic, acting on the liver and the kidneys. You can eat it as a sautéed green or whip it through the blender (once parboiled) and make a creamy nettle/spinach soup. They are called stinging nettles for a reason. Be careful in harvesting this pungent herb. Wear gloves, use pruners. The stings go away once the plant has been cooked. Here's how I take care of my nettle harvest. I have a deep basket that I use to transport them from the place they're cut to my kitchen where they will be processed. I fill a canning-size pot with cold water and I remove the nettles from the basket with long tongs. The tongs are then used to swish the nettles around in the water removing dust and bug bits. I leave them be while I fill another big pot with cold water and set it on the stove to boil. When it has come to a boil, I add the nettles (again with the tongs) to the water and return it to the boil. Then I remove it from the heat, put a lid on it and let the whole mess steep for half a day or more. I decant the tea into half-gallon Mason jars and keep those refrigerated as I use them. You can add honey or other sweetener to the lukewarm tea but I find it tastes best plain. My nettle tea is very dark green and lively.

Mugwort (artemisia vulgaris)

Mugwort, along with rue and vervain, is one of my most-used magical herbs. This is a weed par excellence. It can be drunk as a tea; it can be brewed into a light alcohol ale. I teach my students to use it as a dream tonic. If you are suffering from night terrors, it will bring your dreams down to a manageable level. If you don't remember your dreams, it will clear the path for more recollection. It aids in deep sleeping. I use it dried in sachets and have clients put the sachet inside their pillow. But I prefer it fresh and just cut. I have found another use for this remarkable herb that I want to share with you. I have found it to be both calming and helpful in hospice situations, where loved ones are making the decision to go from us. It's the scent of it, as far as I can tell, so use fresh mugwort, cut and placed in water.

Plantain (plantago major)

Yes, I do have a funny story about being stung on the rear-end by a wasp and then wandering all over my side yard, looking for plantain and holding my aching cheek, only to find my husband had weeded it away. Plantain comes in two varieties around here—broad-leaf and narrow—and both seem to have the same properties. As you may gather from that woeful tale of wasps, it is excellent for use on bug bites, stings and general skin irritation and eruptions. Traditionally, it is picked, wiped off and chewed, then applied directly to the affected area. It is also edible as a spring green but is tough and leathery as the season progresses. It is a weed of great properties and should be encouraged in the healing landscape...and not weeded out. Ahem.

Rabbit Tobacco (pseudognaphalium obtusifolum)

Most country kids at some point in their wicked juvenile careers as stinkers smoked this silvery-green herb because they were told they would get high. It is a ragged little plant that goes easily and messily to seed in the fall, even after harvesting. I use it as part of my Sweet Smoke blend and use it alone as a light incense. In spite of the name, it is not in the tobacco family and does not smell like that. I have found it very helpful as incense that promotes both calm and relaxation and so it is useful for meditation and trance purposes.

Mountain Mint (pycnanthemum virginianum)

I burn this as a cleansing smudge. I understand it can also be smoked to clear the lungs but I have not used it for that. It is the best smelling mint and the scent lingers in the air. I have a big patch of it by the front porch and grown in the garden, it is a prodigious and invasive herb. It grows on woody stems and dies down completely in the winter only to reappear at the first break in the winter weather as tiny curls of green at the bases of the dead stems of the previous year. I use it fresh and dried, and often have some stems of it in my car. Crushed in the palm, it releases a deep fragrance. Burned in a bowl, it releases much the same pleasant smell. I use it to aid in the Sight and to clarify the purpose of workings, either for myself or for a client.

Elderberry (sambucus nigra)

There was a fierce and luxurious blooming of elderberry this year. Since I take so many of my cues from nature, I wonder if that means a nasty cold and flu season is on our horizon. This year, for the first time, I harvested enough of the blossom to create an elderberry cordial and left the rest for making berries. A wise herbalist once told me that one of the great gifts of the Elderberry is her generosity. She makes enough blossom in the spring so that we may take some to use as medicine, in case the berries never form. I have found you can easily have both, if you are careful. And in a good year, like this one, there is a blessed sufficiency.

Queen Ann's Lace (daucus carota)

She is one of the tall beauties of an Appalachian summer but as children we were always warned not to pick them because they had chiggers on them. Chiggers are these teeny-tiny insects that bite you and then burrow into your skin where their very presence sets up an unholy itching. You are supposed to put a dab of fingernail polish on the spot and that will kill the chigger and the itch. This plant is a wild carrot and the seeds have been used traditionally in the southern highlands to prevent pregnancy. I am still superstitious enough to cut the flowers while wearing gloves and to use the seeds or complete flower heads (dried) in sachets. Because of their dainty frilliness, I use them magically in Ancestor work. But please be careful of those chiggers—or you'll wish you were an Ancestor.

Poke or Pokeweed (phytolacca americana)

You may know the song "Poke Salad Annie." Poke (you may hear it called poke sallet around these parts) is a pungent perennial herb that sends up sweet tender leaves in the spring and by frost she is a giant bearing long clumps of juicy purple berries. Birds like those berries and, if you find a streak of bright pink bird-do on your car, you have been sky-tagged by a poke-eating songbird. Poke is toxic and should not be treated carelessly. The early greens may be eaten, but many people find they cause digestive upset. They were a class of "spring tonics" popular here in the mountains. I learned early that poke must cleaned and thrown into boiling salted water. Then drained and the process repeated twice more before they were safe to eat. Long-time poke eaters have told me that's nonsense—you parboil them once then sauté them in butter. I suggest you eat some wilted lettuce and ramps instead. Wilted lettuce is fresh greens over which hot bacon grease has been drizzled. It is good and was my cousin Carl's favorite. Consult a good herbalist about the healing properties of poke (including its fat white root) but until then use the fresh berries to temporarily dye your hair and tattoo your skin. Lay some of the clumps of berries out to dry and use them in sachets to help girls who are approaching their first menses and for women approaching their last. Like red clay, the redness of poke, as well as its strength and resilience, are fine talismans for a woman's Moon time.

Bloodroot (sanguinaria canadensis)

The simple white flower of this native wild plant belies the authority, as well as the color, from the root. But its Latin name tells the story, as they often do. Sanguinaria means blood and a tincture of this root is a sovereign remedy for warts. There are folks here who can rub or talk away warts. I had a great-aunt who could do that. I do not have that gift, so when my daughter got warts on her hand, we tried everything from duct-tape to over-the-counter products to a dermatologist. They just kept coming back. Finally, we hit on bloodroot tincture and that did the trick. Since that time, I've recommended it to many people all of whom have met with good success. You can dig and tincture it yourself but a good health food store can order it for you, if they don't stock it. A little goes a long way, so be ready to share.

Ginseng (panax quinquefolius)

After my first book came out, a good old friend invited me out for coffee. He said he'd read the book and we shared tale after tale of what mountain folks used to do, because he is one, too. At one point he looked at me seriously and said he was puzzled about one thing

I didn't talk about—'sang. Ginseng. I shook my head and told him it was too valuable and endangered now to give anyone ideas about wild harvesting it here. But I can't say too much about the wonder of this little plant in Appalachian history. As I've written about before, much of the land in the southern highlands is thin and poor, and the subsistence farmers who are our Ancestors had to supplement their farming with other cash crops that they sent into town. Firewood, goldenseal, 'sang. It sold and sold and more and more people began to see it as a quick fix for money problems. So it has been over-harvested for a long time now and people are bold and careless enough to go onto national forest land and rustle it. So, I am mentioning it here by way of a historical anecdote and to please Uncle Ted. But don't harvest it unless it grows on your own land. Take only a little of it for your own use and tell no one where it lies. Take only mature plants of three or more prongs. If you have the kind of conditions it needs, contact your local agricultural extension office and seed some of your land with it. That's all. Leave it be.

Gentleman's Walking Stick / Nodding Smartweed (polygonum lapathifolium — or is it persicaria lapathifolium?)

My grandmother was a wealth of odd and curious information. These small pinkish flowers are produced on a stalk, like beads, and when the flowers appear, you know that autumn has come to your land. It took me a long time to discover the proper name of this plant because it is small and humble, but once you see it and can recognize it, it is everywhere in the fall of the year. She told me it was called Gentleman's Walking Stick and I must have questioned why such a little thing was called a walking stick. I'm sure my head was full of notions of tiny faery-men with their knobbly pink walking sticks. My grandmother laughed and remarked casually, "Because sometimes gentlemen have trouble with their walking sticks and then they drink this as a hot tea." I don't pretend that I understood that particular mystery but I remembered what she said and asked her about it later in both our lives. She allowed as how it was mostly for older men who couldn't get their male member to firm up. She hadn't heard of anybody using it in years but remembered hearing about it as a young woman. I don't know if it is still used anywhere for that particular ailment but I know that I use it, dried, in magical work and I use it for protection. It can go into a sachet or little bag. The dried flowers tend to fall off as little beads and if you gather and dry enough of it, you can use it like redding at a doorway or window.

And the reason I have two different botanical names listed? I think the plant she showed me is the persicaria but it isn't native to here. She was probably mis-remembering the polygonum, which is.

The best time to harvest stems, leaves and flowers, generally speaking, is on a waxing Moon, early in the morning. I take a basket or colander out with me, along with some pruners or a sharp knife. Consult the little guide to local plants that we discussed earlier for the best times to harvest. I dry most everything by hanging it from a shelf in the kitchen, though sometimes I lay them on a plastic sheet in the back of the car. When they are dry, I cut or crumble the useable parts and seal them in a resealable plastic bag and a stout canning jar.

This all sounds like a bucolic life in the country but I live in old mill housing on the very edge of a busy downtown. No matter where you live and how much— if any—land you tend, you can practice both foraging and wildcrafting, as well as growing your own. Many city parks have unmanicured edges where a sharp eye may spot plantain and her sisters. It is unlikely they have used weed killer in those areas but a quick call to the Parks Department will let you know. You can do all of this on the down-low, if you choose, but I have found that making acquaintance with the park folks is easy and rewarding. They will often marvel at your desire for stinging nettles or let you know when those wild blackberries are likely to be ripe. Part of practicing a folkway like this is weaving, sometimes reweaving, the fabric of your community. That old retired guy that tends your favorite park may also share some old-time local knowledge about the park itself and all that abides there.

Cities have a surprising amount of wild spaces in them, from overgrown lots to the edges of parking areas. So many of us dream of the little farmstead in the country but many of us due to circumstances mostly beyond our control will always be city-dwellers. I encourage you to live where you are right now and not to postpone the joy of this crafting until you find your ideal rural place. For one thing, you get lots of practice identifying helpful and delicious plant allies. And for another—you may find you never leave the city and you have that dream languish, unfulfilled. Explore your urban resources and see what can be learned, how you can interact with nature in settings that don't seem natural at all. What this requires of you is that you redefine the natural world to mean cracks in concrete and rooftop gardens. It will broaden you and help you to feel at home wherever you may be.

I am, by my nature, a gardener. It could be because

we had a garden when I was growing up or it could be cultural or it could be genetic for all I know. Nature or nurture? There is healing to be found in dirt under the fingernails, in simple acts of clearing away a clump of grass so a good weed can grow. Stress, fear and grief will always drive me to the garden—so will joy, silliness and hunger.

Soil is a living thing, the diverse skin of the planet. If you are fixing to grow a garden, think back to the way we embraced learning about the land we live on, its history, and its story. Now, turn that down a notch and look at the soil beneath your feet. Clay? Sand? Black and friable? Red and lumpy? Does it hold moisture or is it dry and cracked?

I was smiling this morning as I searched amongst the vines for cucumbers ready to be harvested. I would bend low and peer under the big leaves. Cucumbers can be masters of disguise and require a thorough search about three times a week at the height of their producing cycle. Every time I straightened up, a soft grunt mysteriously sounded. Bending again, I picked a beautiful Straight Eight (one of my favorite varieties) and as I straightened, a heard that low grunt. Turns out, it was me. Bend, pick, straighten, grunt. Repeat. Growing a granny garden is not for the weak and if you think all grannies are frail stick-women, you haven't met the old mountain mamas here who have been gardening their whole lives and can take a hoe to a snake like a flash of lightning.

I am not going to give you all the information you need on the art and craft of growing a garden because there are plenty of good books about that subject. Find one whose information includes your region and read up. Then go to the tailgate market in your town and talk to the folks that grow all that pretty food. You can learn more in a relaxed conversation with a gardener than you might think. But make sure and buy some of that local produce in exchange for information. It would be bad manners to take up a vendor's time and not make some sort of exchange, now, wouldn't it?

But I am going to tell you some of the traditional vegetables that are raised on the hill farms of southern Appalachia and then we'll go over some of the other things that a person with an eye toward magic work might consider getting into the ground.

When I was coming up, the family garden didn't hold a wide variety of vegetables but it held a lot of them. Tomatoes, a couple of varieties of corn (for eating, milling, livestock feed), green beans, cucumbers, onions, carrots, mustard greens, okra. You might have turnips (for the greens and the roots) and beets (the same). In the fall and early spring, we'd grow collard greens. Collards love cool weather and are very delicious to insects.

It seems like every year, someone would find something unusual in a seed catalog and order it just for fun. We grew kohlrabi one year but it didn't turn out very well. We didn't grow things like spinach, broccoli, kale or pak choi but we did grow cabbages that were then made into spicy chow-chow that we ate on beans in the winter. We didn't grow a whole lot of peppers, but my cousin Bosie grew some that were hot called "peter peppers" because of their shape.

And we grew hills of white potatoes—Arsh (Irish) potatoes—that kept pretty well over the winter. We weren't dedicated gardeners like many of our neighbors. But my daddy had a job and we had access to store-bought food, too. In his last years, after he and my mother had moved into town, he would visit a buddy who had a tomato farm and late in the growing season, he'd buy a couple of boxes of green tomatoes. He took them home, wrapped each individual tomato in newspaper, and hauled the boxes down to the basement. He'd lose some of them over the course of the winter but was often rewarded with those slow-ripening fruits well into the new year.

Roots crops are planted in the dark of the Moon (as the Moon is waning) and above-ground crops in the light of the Moon (as it is waxing to full). The Moon's phase was important but also what astrological sign it was in. I am not an astrologer, let me be clear on that.

I have good friends who are and they advise me about the niceties of the stars. If you, like I, do not have the gift of the stars, I suggest you find an astrologer you trust and can talk to. And every year, get yourself a farmer's almanac to keep you informed. I also recommend "Raising by the Moon" by Jack Pyle and Taylor Reese. It is a treasure-trove of useful information and they are very nice men, too.

Some almanacs will advise you to do certain things when "the signs are in" a particular body part. Here's a quick rundown of what that means.

Aries rules the head and is a barren Fire sign, good for harvesting root crops and destroying weeds.

Taurus rules the neck and is a moist and productive Earth sign. Good for planting, transplanting.

Gemini rules the arms and is a barren Air sign. Good for cultivating and getting rid of pests.

Cancer is a fertile Water sign and rules the breast. It is believed to be the best sign for planting and for grafting.

Leo is a barren, dry Fire sign and rules the heart. It is a good sign for tidying up in the garden, including killing weeds and insect pests.

Virgo rules the bowels and is a warm and moist Earth sign. Good for flowers and soil improvement.

Libra is a moist and fruitful Air sign that rules the reins. Good for planting fragrant crops—flowers, herbs and the like.

Scorpio rules secrets and is a fertile Water sign. Good for planting perennials and setting seed for large plants like corn and squash.

Sagittarius is a barren Fire sign and rules the thighs. Onions dug in this sign will keep well in storage and it's a good time to plant trees.

Capricorn rules our achy knees—a dry though productive Earth sign. Good for pruning and amending the soil, and for root crops.

Aquarius is a dry, barren Air sign. Good time to get rid of weeds and insect pests and to put fruit into storage.

Pisces rules the feet and is a moist and fertile Water sign. Excellent for planting.

This is a simple rundown of the signs and their associations. For more detailed information, go out and get yourself an almanac.

You didn't pick up a book on folk magic to learn how to grow green beans, so here's the Other Part of your granny garden. Some of these plants should come with a warning label so be mindful of who can access this part of your garden. The following plants are used for energy work and should not be ingested.

Vervain (verbena officinalis)

I use vervain, which is not native to western North Carolina, for weather work, specifically storm-calling. I have a little patch of it in the corner of my main garden and I dry it for use in the winter. Vervain oil is easy to make and easy to use. I lay it down on dark Moon and have a strong batch that was laid down during a solar eclipse as well—it's Dark Moon/Dark Sun Vervain Oil.

Rue (ruta graveolens)

Rue, the Amazing Rue! She is a powerful plant and a good ally but you must be very careful in the handling of her. She has been used as an abortifacient herb and handling the plant itself can cause nasty skin irritation. If you do not know how your skin reacts to rue, you must always wear gloves when handling the plant, even after it is dried. I make rue oil for candles and for other dressing and you must also be careful when handling rue oil, if you haven't handled it before. A box of disposable latex gloves will be your friend. I use rue magically to rid myself of what no longer serves or nourishes me. I used some dried when I was trying to break myself from eating processed sugar, which I love but does not love me. I put it in a sachet and kept the sachet with me, either in pocket or purse. It worked for many months before that Demon Sugar returned to claim my weak, pie-loving soul. Then I did the process again because six months without sugar is a very good thing—even when I have to repeat the process twice a year.

I also use rue oil or dried rue as a kind of rocket fuel for any kind of working I'm doing. Even if a working starts with a different kind of dressing oil, I always add a little dab of the rue as a kickstarter. I also have seven-day (glass jar) candles that are infused with rue and I light those during workings or when I want to focus on a sick or needful friend.

Nightshade (atropa belladonna)

I had a tremendous nightshade plant as a neighbor when I was visiting Glastonbury a few years back and it got me to thinking I'd like one in my garden, since there are not children visiting here now. I have a potted one that I'll put in the ground in the fall and will watch to keep it out of reach of curious hands. The berries are so beautiful, you see, so tempting. I ate some when I was a child but ate the green ones and suffered no ill effects. But twenty years ago when I was looking for a preschool for my daughter, we visited one that seemed a good fit. The director had to take a call while we were there and we wandered around the playground where there were shards of some hard plastic from a broken toy. Strike Number One, in the safety department. The fence was covered with a glorious and suspicious growth and I stepped closer to identify it. At that moment the director returned, apologizing for neglecting us. She noticed my focus. "Isn't that beautiful? It comes back every year and it gets bright red berries in the fall that turn purple." I continued to look at the luxurious plant. "Do you know what this is?" I asked. She didn't. "It's deadly nightshade. Atropa belladonna." I will leave you to imagine her reaction. I merely advised her to wear gloves when she dug it up. Needless to say, my daughter went to preschool elsewhere.

Do not ingest this. Do not ingest this. Do not ingest this. And handle it with extreme caution, while wearing gloves. Don't rub your eyes, pick your teeth or your nose after handling this beautiful lady. I use it in sachets and sometimes in egg bindings, to really make my point. It can be used energetically (dried in a sachet) for dealing with addictions or breaking toxic relationships.

Jimson Weed (datura stramonium)

This plant has large trumpet-flowers and is very pretty in your garden. It can be invasive so keep an eye on it. You'll only need one or two for your work. I don't like the name Jimson weed so I call it by its proper name—Datura. I harvest the seed pods, which are about hen egg-sized, and hen egg-shaped but covered with sharp spikes. It splits as it is drying and reveals black seeds. I collect the entire seed head and use it in banework. It is good for protecting the innocent (yes, sometimes you may choose to protect the guilty but that is your business). It is good for warding off people who mean you or yours harm. And it looks wicked when displayed in a jar with the lid on tight. Wash your hands after handling and do not ingest. Keep it out of reach of everyone because you—like everybody else—know people stupid enough to think it would be cool to take something called "loco weed."

Flowering Tobacco (nicotiana)

This is one of the plants beloved of the land spirits and other spirit-folk. There is an old variety that is night-blooming and fragrant, if you can find that. It is a self-seeding perennial in our zone and has a strong yellow root system. It lives in the fenced off garden we call the Italian Garden and blooms with small white trumpets every year. I take the leaves in the late summer and early fall and dry them. They are then burned as a sacred smoke to honor the Land Folks as well as the Ancestors.

Hellebore (helleborus niger, helleborus foetida)

These are very odd plants. They bloom when other things aren't blooming and the blooms last for weeks. I have two varieties—one that blooms in the early winter with tiny green flowers (foetida) and the one that blooms in spring (niger) and is called the Lenten Rose. Like nicotiana, these are beloved of the Gentry and of shy land spirits that seem to congregate under the thick leaves. I grow them in the garden for those reasons and I harvest and dry leaves for use on Ancestor altars. There is a superstition (not an Appalachian one) that you should never cut and dry the flowers for use. You may cut them and bring some inside to enjoy but they should return to nature when they droop and die. I abide by that superstition though it is not culturally traditional.

The ones listed below are also culinary or tea herbs but we will be talking about their energetic and magical properties:

Lavender (lavandula angustifolia)

Such an important plant for all kinds of healing. It is used fresh, dried, in oil, in water. It can be difficult to grow because people often pamper it too much. It likes poor soil and not too much water. It likes plenty of space in which to stretch out and it needs to be cut and used often. It goes into sachets to remind us of our connection to all good things. It will calm most people and is often used in sickrooms as well as nurseries. Use it for everything that requires a gentle but firm healing touch. Use it in combination with rosemary and meditation to do your own deep work on healing your memories.

Rosemary (rosmarinus officinalis)

According to Shakespeare and English tradition (which is where he stole the idea), rosemary is for remembrance. Plant it for your Ancestors and use the diluted essential oil on Ancestor altars. It can also be used to help you remember. When you are having a low day and your own self-esteem is in the ditch with the tadpoles, use rosemary (either fresh or diluted oil) as part of your meditation or prayer time. Remember who you are and allow all the pieces of your good, strong self to reemerge as you breathe deeply.

Catnip (nepeta cataria)

O, how I love this great monstrous mint. The kitties love it, of course, but harvested young it makes a potent tea that helps new breastfeeding mothers relax and gives them more milk. It is calming to the point of soporific. It can be added as an oil to an emollient base and used as a cream for massaging the temples of people prone to migraines. I pick it long, hang it up for several days until it dries, and crumble it into a large jar or ziplock bag.

Lemon Balm (melissa officianalis)

We cut great bouquets of this in the Women's Garden and hang it to dry. It makes a relaxing and refreshing tea.

If you love the soil in your growing patch and tend it with care, it will reward you with good things to eat, and relaxing time getting your hands dirty. It is hard work and good exercise. Remember to plant above-ground crops in the light of the Moon and below-ground crops in the dark of the Moon. Keep the ground weeded and mulched, and don't overwater.

But you may not be so lucky as to have land of your own and common land that can be harvested. And there are so many wonderful reasons to have a garden of your own. If you don't have space for a garden, check your area for community gardens that can use your help in exchange for a little land to plant for yourself. And, if all else fails, make yourself a container garden. Working the soil is a magical thing and imparts a kind of healing you will get nowhere else.

The long evenings of summer and the brisk mornings of early spring and late autumn are threshold times when one may encounter magic in the land. When we answer a summons from the Mother, we are likely to step into places that are terribly familiar and terribly unknown. Only you can know what delights await you as you forage and grow, tend and harvest.

Receipt for Oil of Rue or Oil of Vervain

Pick the fresh herb in the morning, when the Moon is beginning to wax. Fill a small canning jar or recycled jar three-quarters full of whichever herb you are using. Fill the jar with inexpensive cooking-grade oil. Let set for a Moon cycle, shaking often. At the end of the Moon cycle, decant the oil and keep it in a cool, dark place. In hot weather, you may see some mold on the green bits. Since you remove those at the end of the process—and because this oil is never ingested—the mold isn't a problem.

Chapter Seven

An Old-Timey Medicine Chest

When I am waiting for a prescription to be filled at my local pharmacy, I wander through the aisles of over-the-counter medications. Sometimes I am rewarded with some fascinatingly old-fashioned remedy that I have never seen or heard of before. I will sometimes ask the nice pharmacist lady if she's ever used whatever it is. She usually shakes her head, no. They are very patient with me there, as you can tell.

I actually have an old medicine chest, hanging near the fireplace in my dining room. It is backless and doorless with lingering streaks of old paint. When I was little, it held the china horses I got at French's Five and Dime but it belonged to my great- grandmother—on my mother's side, as I recall. The long edges are carved into twists and it now holds bits of family treasure: the Blessed Virgin whose wings are shells and is a nightlight and a bottle that once resided in the glove compartment of my grandparent's Cadillac where it held protective Holy Water.

Its contents would have been quite different when it hung on the wall at Number Ten Roberts Street. It might have held some patent medicines, a glass eyewash cup, a bottle of Mercurochrome and some paregoric. These oddments of medicine took the place of today's corner drugstore and were indispensable throughout the southern highlands.

Other possible items might include tincture methylate, Epsom salts and ipecac. What wouldn't be on those little shelves are the various home remedies that were made as needed, usually from ingredients that were close at hand, either in the yard or the kitchen. This chapter is an excursion into popular patent medicines of the not-so-distant past but it's mostly about the herbs and dirts and animal parts that regular folks used—and still use—for various ailments and maladies. We'll also consider the double uses of these remedies in what I often call the "spirit-haunted landscape of the South."

Let's start with some logical divisions and definitions.

Tonics, syrups and draughts are taken internally and generally contain alcohol, though some "spring tonics" were herbal mixtures that are cooked up and eaten.

Lotions and liniments are applied externally and are thin, rubbed into the skin.

Poultices are applied externally and are often thick, viscous and lumpy. They are sometimes contained in a cloth, preferably flannel. The same flannel could be used to make a small pouch to wear around the neck to prevent an illness or relieve symptoms.

Many of the ailments that plagued my rural

Appalachian Ancestors are easily dealt with in modern times, if we can afford it. Drug stores stock remedies for intestinal worms, diarrhea, constipation, skin irritations, and minor wounds. The way we live has changed, too, from housing to regular dental check-ups. We mostly have hot water on demand now and flush toilets, and our days are not filled with the hazards of farm living—snake bite, rabid animals, accidental amputation, third degree burns from kerosene lamps and wood cook stoves.

As a woman, I often think about the harsh realities of life in a world where you had little or no control over your reproductive life, because the culture demanded many children and there was no way of knowing how many would reach adulthood. Mountain women have used—and some still use—wild carrot seed as a birth control method but any natural method requires strict attention to both your body and the calendar by both parties in baby-making. The Protestant structure of family life made it near impossible for a woman to say no to her husband when it came to intimate matters. Maternal death in childbirth was hardly a rare thing. Visit any old cemetery and note the stones where a man remarried after a wife died in childbirth, leaving behind children that must be raised. He'd choose a new partner and the cycle continued. Between a Biblical insistence on a husband's authority, a high infant mortality rate and the lack of reliable birth control, a rural woman at the turn of the last century got married young (often as young as fifteen or sixteen) and she spent her life pregnant, nursing and tending children. My maternal great-grandmother died in her seventies from complications of a broken hip. In a family portrait from 1904, her nine living children, who range in age from adult to infant, surround her and she is pregnant with her last child. She is forty-three years old.

As you might imagine, childbirth and "women's complaints" have many patent medicine choices. I love the phrase "women's complaints." Given the kind of life our foremothers lived—up before dawn, laundering by hand, tending a garden, feeding the chickens and gathering eggs, canning for winter, making clothes, cooking on a wood stove, all while pregnant or nursing or otherwise dealing with little children. No wonder they had complaints and took to their beds on occasion. There weren't vacations then, you know. That was her life. As children grew, the older boys would help in the field or work in the mill and the girls would help out in the house or work in the mill. They might have gone to school, especially the boys, but they might not have. The mother of the house would have some help then but there were also more mouths to feed, more clothes to sew. Even on Sunday—the so-called day of rest in Christian households—the family had to be fed and sorted out for a trip to church. The afternoon often saw a big meal with extended family and a big meal always ended with a big clean up. Then the week would begin again, same as it ever was.

If you read about patent medicines of the time, you'll find all sorts of answers to these women's complaints, most of which include alcohol, or drugs like cocaine or opium. The medicines were simply bottled cocktails and they may indeed have made a woman feel better because she felt less stressed and hopeless. They were available from traveling salesmen and were often just the right size to fit in a woman's apron pocket. For cultural reasons, the woman wasn't allowed to drink alcohol for pleasure but she was allowed patent medicines that would deal with her illnesses—her headaches, her nervousness, her irritability, her female troubles. The woman was allowed this expenditure in a time when there wasn't much cash-money because it was thought to help the entire family. When Mama felt good, she was happier with her life and that made family life better for all concerned. And if that took some of her butter-and-eggs money, that was only fair.

Mama also served as the family doctor and had an arsenal of medicines for wounds and other maladies. Cobwebs were used to stop bleeding on minor cuts but a big flow of blood might require murmuring a particular Bible verse over the wound. My step-grandfather, who was from Georgia, had the knack for that—stopping a flow of blood. My mother used to tell of the time she called him on the phone to stop the bleeding on a cut. He said the verse (which was kept secret) and the bleeding stopped. So did her period. I have since learned that the most often used verse for staunching blood is Ezekiel 16:6. Here it is from the King James Version, the only one a self-respecting mountain person would ever use, "And when I passed by thee, and saw thee polluted in thine own blood, I said unto thee when thou wast in thy blood, Live; yea, I said unto thee when thou wast in thy blood, Live."

The peril of impending childbirth required many preparations. Children were born at home, often in the same bed where they were conceived. A stone with a naturally occurring stone—a holey stone—might be hanging from a string in the east-facing window. Anything in the room that was tied (shoe laces, bodices and the like) was all untied and the woman's hair was loosened. This sympathetic magic was believed to loosen her womb and make childbirth safer and easier. A cast-iron pan with a small knife in it was sometimes placed under the bed, the knife there to cut the pain.

Below are some commonly used Appalachian treatments for healing various ailments, some homemade, some store-bought. (These are offered as memories of by-gone days. I am not a doctor or even an herbalist. I am merely reporting what used to be offered by way of treatments.)

You can find most of these at the drugstore and you should take a look at them, if only for the pretty labels and list of ingredients.

Black draught is a laxative, made with senna and magnesia.

BenGay and Cornhuskers lotion are both very smelly and moderately effective salves for muscle ache and skin irritations.

The combination of camphor and menthol is a very old treatment for a variety of ailments. It is available in several commercial products including Carmex, Camphophenique, Mentholatum and Vicks VapoRub. The beneficial action of camphor and menthol work for nasal congestion, skin irritations and small wounds, minor burns and fever blisters. Camphorated oil or camphor oil is the bark of the camphor tree in an oily base.

I ran into a product called Astyptodyne, a pine oil liniment, at the Mast General Store in Boone, NC. The story of how it came to be is very interesting and I have found it to be good on minor burns. I sometimes use it in conjunction with the Burn Spell, which we covered in a previous chapter.

Carbolated petroleum jelly (Vaseline) used to be a must-have in the medicine cabinet. You can still get it in places where you find Watkins Products. Used to protect burns and cuts, the addition of phenyl gave it a reputation for wound—and especially burn—healing.

There are many materials that are known for their "drawing ability," a necessity for the sorts of carbuncles, splinters and sores that are part and parcel of living in the country. You want to draw out the poison, the pus, and the sliver of stovewood that makes the side of your hand sore. Black drawing salve, which is sometimes called by its actual name ichthammol, is a nasty, greasy salve used on boils, splinters, bug bites and stings to draw out the infection. I have found it to work but don't wear your good clothes while treating yourself with this over-the-counter medicine. I prefer grated raw potato myself, which is discussed below.

Castor oil has become a cultural byword for mean things your parents did to make you feel better and that you resent forever. It was, and sometimes still is, given for tummy troubles and also when a child is unruly and obnoxious.

A few drops of sweet oil are used for a mild earache. Sweet oil is olive oil. It is available in a small bottle at the drugstore but a few drops of food grade olive oil from the kitchen will also help ease the pain.

The ones that follow are homemade remedies. I have noted where I have tried them and whether or not it worked.

In addition to the drawing salve mentioned previously, another means of drawing out infection is a poultice made from raw white potato. My dad came back from World War II with a fungus on his feet that was often treated but not cured. It made his feet very itchy and flaky. Someone—one of our neighbors, I reckon—told me about grated raw potato and we tried it. It gave him relief from the symptoms but the fungus didn't go completely away until he swam in the ocean off the Isle of Palms in South Carolina. The poultice turns black as the potato is oxidized in the air, by the way. Don't be alarmed by the dramatic change.

I have not tried kerosene with sugar as a cure for sore throat and I certainly do not recommend you ingest kerosene. But it was popular in home remedies during the Depression. Kerosene was also used to keep bedbugs away during that same time period. The legs of an iron bedstead were set into short cans containing kerosene. Yes, kerosene. I've been told that was done but I haven't been told if it worked. Don't try it though, for the modern recurrence of this pest, even if you do sleep in an iron bedstead.

Honey, rock candy, and whiskey mixed in a snuff glass are a sovereign treatment for a cold with a cough. I wish I had a better receipt for it than this but I don't. Put a pinch of rock candy in the bottom of the glass; add a shot of whiskey and a heaping spoonful of honey. Stir until it thickens up and the candy dissolves. Take by the teaspoonful. You may choose to adjust the amounts of each. It is good for a cough. I have tried it.

My maternal great-grandmother swore by horehound candy for sore throats and to clear the throat. They are readily available these days as an "old-timey" candy and they do soothe a sore throat. I have never tried it as a substitute for rock candy in the previous receipt but I reckon that might work.

The common cold is an apt description. Nowadays, we hardly slow down when we get one and the average person gets a couple of them every year. We go to the drug store and get something for the cough and something for the sore throat and something for the aches. Mountains remedies for colds are less dependent on over-the-counter remedies and have some strange components.

We were always rubbed down the chest and throat with Vicks VapoRub, which replaced the mustard poultice of previous generations. It is generally believed that wearing a dirty sock around your neck will take away a sore throat. I have a cousin who swears that getting into a hot shower and washing your hair will cure a cold. But here is the best remedy I have found for it and I take this every day when I have a bad cold.

Fried Onions: Chop up the stinkiest onion you have. Those big yellow ones are generally best. Some big sweet onion from Georgia will do you no good at all. Put some grease in a cast-iron pan. I usually use olive oil (not traditional, for sure) but bacon drippings, butter or chicken fat will also work. Cook the onions long and slow, until they are clear and starting to crisp at the edges.

I add in a lot of garlic (not traditional). The kitchen smells wonderful, if you have your smeller working. Now add in some strong black pepper and stir it all up.

At about this time, I put in an egg or two to bind it all together. Dash of salt on top. Eat it while it's hot, as hot as you can stand.

There will come a point in a couple of days when the thought of one more dish of onions is not appealing. That means the virus has been defeated and you can stop the delicious remedy. And maybe take a nice hot shower and wash your hair.

My grandmother swore that eating sugar made you susceptible to colds and refrained from that, but never quit it entirely. She was healthy for most of her long life and we know sugar is bad for you, so maybe switch to local raw honey for your sweetness, unless you are sweet enough without it.

Kissing a redhead can cure a cold sore or fever blister, or so they say.

Every time I mention the name of this book to people in the know, they back away as soon as they hear the word "asfidity." Then the tales start. Oh, mercy, what a smell! Asfidity is correctly spelled asafoetida and it is an ingredient used in Indian cuisine, very sparingly. It became popular at the turn of the last century, in the Golden Age of Patent Medicines, as a cure for all sorts of ailments, primarily respiratory ones. When the Spanish flu devastated the region at about the time of the First World War, asfidity was believed to protect the wearer from it. That particular strain of influenza was especially hard on pregnant women (who almost always died if infected) and new mothers and babies, so asfidity bags were everywhere then.

It was sold in chunks and a piece would be broken off and put in a little cotton bag that was worn around the neck on a string. Various other things would go into the bag with it—little talismans for good health. These talismans varied across the region but often included a penny, a small nail, a shard of broken mirror or piece of mica, a bit of honeycomb, and some mud dauber nest.

One of the things that they almost always contained was something shiny and a little ragged—the mica or mirror shard. This was important for the other general use of asfidity bags. In addition to repelling disease-casing germs, it was also promoted as a way to repel the interest of and interference from haints and other wandering spirits. I am pretty sure that asfidity didn't keep away influenza, though it may have kept your contact with other folks to a bare minimum because of the smell. But I am intrigued about repelling spirits and am sure we have no way to determine whether that is a successful working. I offer it here as a cultural tidbit.

Bites from animals (including snakes) are still a risk in the world at large but especially in the country. A drawing salve or poultice would be used to draw out the "pizen" and drinking alcohol poured into the wounds. A snake or spider bite can turn bad pretty quickly and great attention would have been paid.

I've told the story of mad-stones elsewhere—and their alleged secret power over sexually-transmitted diseases. Mad-stones were also kept in case of a bite by a rabid animal. Rubbing the wound with the calcified nub out of a deer's stomach was said to have curative powers —that the stone would draw out the infection. The stone had to be boiled in milk before use and had to be tended lovingly between uses. A holler might only have one and it would be passed from person to person, as the need arose.

One remedy I do offer to folks is blackberry jam for diarrhea. It works very well and is delicious, too. You may make it yourself after a day of berry-picking up at the Bald or you can buy some at the grocery store.

Cherry Bark Cough Syrup

The best way to harvest bark is to prune smaller branches from the tree with secateurs/pruning shears. A good handful of prunings will yield enough bark for most receipts (the traditional word for "recipes"). Never take bark from the trunk of a tree. Best times to harvest are spring and fall, as the leaves are changing. Use a vegetable peeler or good knife to whittle off the bark. Fill a quart Mason jar with this fresh cherry bark. Fill the remaining space with vodka or rum. Leave it for a Moon cycle. Strain out the liquid and add an equal amount of local raw honey. Simmer gently until the honey has liquefied, then simmer another five minutes. Most of the alcohol will have evaporated, by the way. Don't give this to babies or very small children because of the issues around honey and the very young. Store in a dark container, preferably in the fridge. Tasty and soothing. This can also be added to warm water to make a tea. Coughs are often accompanied by a sore throat, so warm is good.

Chapter Eight

Working with the Dead: Haints, Ancestors and the Beloved Dead

I grew up in a world rich with spirits—from the ghost of Mr. Haney to the legend of the ghost-man who slept upstairs in the house where my grandmother was born. In fairness to her, I must credit my mother with many of the stories that shaped my knowledge of the spiritual remnants of the dead. She seemed to have a knack for experiencing them and certainly had a way of telling of them that has stuck with me through all these long years.

Rural people used to refer to these as "haints"—the dead who stick around in spirit long after their flesh has gone into the old earth. They are our spirit-kin and, when I was growing up, everyone believed in the existence of ghosts and most people had a tale to tell about something that really really happened.

In this chapter, I'll share a few of those tales and histories, write a little about ways to settle a restless one, and then touch on the care and keeping of burial places, including the old traditions around Decoration Day.

The neighborhood where I live now and where

I've lived since the 1980s is also the place where my grandmother and mother grew up. When my mother and father married and he moved her to that drafty little house at the head of the cove, she often spoke wistfully, or at least it seems that way to me now, about the house where her mother grew up and where she spent time as a child.

Its address was also its name and so Number Ten Roberts Street figures prominently in my Ancestor-laden imagination. We have photos of the exterior. The first floor was a neighborhood grocery store, Westmoreland Grocery, and the family lived upstairs and in the back of the store. It was on the second floor that the ghost of a man slept on an old couch. He slept with his back to the room and was most easily visible when the glow of the streetlamp brightened the room. He was an object of curiosity, no more than that, and it was this casual attitude toward these old haints that has colored my ongoing work with the spirits of the dead.

The ghost of one of my grandmother's sisters was not met with such calm acceptance. This particular great-aunt had a weak heart and my mother always believed that she had caused her auntie to have a fatal heart attack by throwing a rubber snake in her lap. She also knew that she was whipped a few weeks later when she came inside the house to tell her mother that she had seen her dead aunt "floating on a cloud."

There must've been some sort of prohibition about seeing deceased family members, or was she punished because she was thought to be lying, or because her story re-traumatized a family already steeped in the grief of its loss? If she ever knew, she never told me. It has become one of those family myths that is filled with sadness, confusion, and a deep sense of how hard their lives were then, here in this neighborhood where I raised my own daughter to adulthood.

My parents moved out to the country in the early years of their marriage, after my father had returned from World War II. They moved into a rough little house on lovingly tended land. The house had a deep front porch roof that looked like "an old man in a billed cap" according to my mother who didn't like it because it made the house too dark. My father and his friends tore the porch off the house and in my day the front door had a simple concrete stoop in front of it.

The old couple from whom they'd bought the place were Mr. and Mrs. Haney and they were related to the people down the hill from us. Mr. Haney made a habit of visiting the house often and, after his death, my mom would sometimes still hear him clearing his throat and could smell the smoke from his cigarette. Mr. Haney was gone—really gone this time—by the time I was old enough to hear the story from my mother.

The haint with whom I lived the longest was Mrs.

Brown and this haint had (or rather has) a long and complicated history. When my grandmother and step-grandfather bought a two-story house in one of our prominent historic neighborhoods, my father helped with the move, with painting and some other odd jobs to get the old house ready. On more than one occasion, he was rewarded for his help by having a flat tire when he came out to the car to come home. My grandmother promptly decided that the resident ghost, Mrs. Brown, didn't like men.

This was further substantiated when my grandmother's oldest brother came down from New York to visit the family in North Carolina. He slept in the guestroom, which was called the back bedroom. It had a disused fireplace with a mantle full of bric-a-brac. As he sat up in bed, reading, one night, he noticed movement out of the corner of his eye and looked up. A milk glass vase of blue plastic flowers rose from the mantle and flew across the room, smashing against the wall near my great-uncle's bald head. I can't remember the details of his reaction but forever after the incident was referred to as "the time Mrs. Brown threw a vase at Uncle Carl."

Mrs. Brown was quite the prankster when my grandparents were alive and was very active when I lived with them while attending the local college. I slept in the back bedroom but never had the kind of dramatic encounter that marked Uncle Carl's visit. Sometimes, on a hot summer night, you could hear a distinct thud-thud-thud down the stairs to the second floor, ending with a resounding THUD at the bottom. We were given to believe—I assume by my grandmother, though I can't strictly speaking recall—that Mrs. Brown had fallen down those stairs years before, broken her hip, and had died in the back bedroom.

My parents moved in after my grandfather died and lived there with my grandmother until she, in turn, passed away. And after my father and then my mother died, my brother and his family moved into the old house.

And that's when it got interesting.

My sister-in-law also heard and occasionally saw the ghost, this "Mrs. Brown." She started doing research on previous owners of the house and she found out there had, indeed, been a previous owner named Brown who had lived there. But it was Mr. Brown and he hadn't died in the house at all.

Book-learning, as it always turns out, can be a very handy thing.

She still sometimes sees the figure of a young man in overalls, standing in the dining room and looking out the front window. The first time she encountered him, she assumed it was her eldest son and paid the apparition no attention at all. Until she realized he hadn't worn overalls in years and was, in fact, at work. I still wonder about the thud-thud-thud sometimes and wonder what in the world that was.

We want to believe in these spirit-kin. Every culture has tales about them and ways to interact with and honor them. Our mountain culture is no different. There are some Protestant groups that don't hold with such nonsense and are liable to call any sort of ghostly visitation something "demonic." But most of the people I know and have talked with who are deeply part of this culture have a soft spot for the lore and mystery that surround our discarnate neighbors.

For the most part, the live-and-let-live attitude of mountain people also applies to the formerly living. As long as haints don't sour the milk or make the baby cry, people are content to let them play out their assigned role and to carry on the tale of their passing and presence.

I was called to a house very near my neighborhood to see what I made of the resident ghost. I walked through the upstairs where I remarked on a couple of cold spots and an area that seemed very bouncy. (I use "bouncy" to refer to space that seems to have a particular energy signature that implies spiritual activity. It's a friendly euphemism that's cheery to the faint-hearted.) The owner told me that the ghost had been seen on many occasions crossing the hall at exactly the places I'd remarked on being cold. We went downstairs and talked about some of the sightings. Like my sister-in-law, this client had done some homework and knew her name and a little of her history. He spoke as fondly of her as if she was his eccentric maiden auntie.

Since he had brought me into the house and regaled me with her legacy, I wondered what my place was in the story and asked him what he wanted me to do about her. Do? He looked puzzled. I only wanted you to confirm that all this is happening. We love her and, well, it's her house really. We don't want her to go.

That about sums it up. We love them and we mostly don't want them to go.

When you or your client need a rambling spirit to keep on rambling, there are several things you can do: bell and anoint the house, set an energy trap, or jar them.

Bell and Anoint the House

This is a basic house cleansing with added attention paid to the Unseen Resident. I ask the homeowner to open all doors and windows, if possible. I leave an offering outside for the land spirits and then spend a few minutes of quiet time, explaining to the Unseen Resident that it is time for her to go on home to her family. If I know her name, I address her by name. I usually do this silently and finish by announcing aloud,

"Time to do the house."

I walk through the house, starting at the front door. I carry a pot of sweet smoke, using my open hand to waft it into all the corners. I do every room—front to back, basement to attic. This can take a while if it's a big house so leave yourself plenty of time to do a thorough job.

I pass through the house a second time, this time ringing a large bell. I used to use my great-grandmother's dinner bell but I bought a small cowbell a few years ago and that sets up a racket, which is a good thing. Often I'll ask the owners to step outside because the effects of the ringing can be unpleasant. In fact, if you do this very often, you may want to use ear protection yourself. I keep little green earplugs in my little black bag.

I do a third and final pass through in which I dab a drop of oil on the door jams, window sills, fireplace, sinks—all the openings into (and out of) the house that I can reach. I do this one slowly, too, and I begin again at the front door by placing my hand on the side of the open door and saying firmly, "Bless this house and all who enter here."

When I have finished all the dressing-and-blessing work, I go to stand at the back door and wish the departing spirit a loving farewell and a safe journey home. Let me stress that this can take a couple of hours to do properly—longer if you are inexperienced—and you don't want to do a lick-and-a-promise job here. You can also invite the homeowner to stand with you for the final farewell part. That can be surprisingly touching and involving your client will help them to establish their claim to be the only resident.

Another tactic I've used is a trap made out of a jar with a lid, which is half-filled with soil. I have found this to be especially useful with an unknown or disruptive spirit energy. Depending on the size of the job, I set up the jar in the lowest point of the building that I can access. I place a battery-operated tealight candle on top of the soil and then I spend my quiet time as I explained in Bell and Anoint. I leave the jar open for three or seven days, depending on my schedule, the schedule of the client and the size of the job. (I ask the client to check on it daily and replace the tealight if it burns out.) At the end of that time, I place the lid on the jar as tightly as it can be twisted. I remove the jar of soil with the tealight still glowing and then take the whole thing to a suitable cemetery. I pour the soil out at the edge of the cemetery and extinguish the light. I take the jar and tealight with me, leaving only some soil behind in an out-of-the-way place.

Several years ago, my city decided to tear down an old building, an historic part of the fabric of the town, to put up a new jail. This building was being used as the Board of Elections office but its former life had seen it as a mediation center and before that a funeral home. The old-fashioned kind with a big picture window in the front, do you remember those? I was so annoyed with the decision to demolish it that I went to the front of the building and invited all its Unseen Residents (whom I had heard were numerous) to follow me down to the county courthouse. To make a long story short, I "installed" them in the elevators there. Lawyer friends who spend time in the courthouse have reported that the activity is noticeable, especially in the one on the left.

The late Vine Deloria once wrote that when the bones of our Ancestors are buried in the land, then we belong to that land, too. For rural mountain people who still live in the places where their families have lived for generations, there is an understanding of the duty that is owed the dead. Family graveyards still sit astride lonely hilltops, settled above cabins and farmhouses, overlooking the ruins of chimneys and tobacco barns. If you travel out Reems Creek and turn right onto Ballard Branch, you will soon find, over to your left, a little burying ground bounded by a short metal fence. There are plenty of Ballards there: not my direct Ancestors but they are some sort of cousins-once-removed. It's an old place, lovingly tended.

In the South, we do that tending in an official kind of way when we celebrate Decoration Day once a year. The date of Decoration Day varies somewhat by location but it is usually held on a Sunday afternoon in summer or at harvest time. It is often connected to a church with its own graveyard stretched out behind the main building and there is sometimes a covered dish supper and singing. Folks bring clippers and trowels and work gloves and the grounds are trimmed and pruned and tended. If you are very lucky or well connected, there is also some perfectly fried chicken or a bowl of real banana pudding or spice cake with old-fashioned boiled frosting.

It's becoming rarer now but it used to be that graves were tended on other special days as well. There would be small flags from the VFW for the resting places of old soldiers and at Easter, Christmas and the Fourth of July, the resting places boasted seasonally appropriate plastic floral arrangements, one for each stone. There might be toys on the graves of children, brought by their grieving family as an act of birthday love. Fat and potted chrysanthemums still come out in the fall and it isn't unusual at all to see a little tree on the family plot come the middle of December.

Several years ago, some friends were making a nighttime run for supplies from our festival spot in middle Tennessee. It was a clear night and part of their journey took them past a wide and sloping cemetery. As they drove past the area, they noticed tiny lights in a fairly regular pattern. Not remembering the cemetery, they thought for a moment it was some sort of landing strip for a private plane. Then they realized where they were and started to feel a little creeped out—before they realized the ghostly lights were solar path lights that folks had pushed into the ground near the markers for their loved ones' grave. I find it touching that there was a desire to illuminate the place after dark. Were they trying to light up the headstones or were they leaving soothing nightlights for the dead?

These are old traditions, some made new, and they speak of the kind of respect for the dead that borders on Ancestor veneration, though most folks around here wouldn't hold with such a notion. When we look through old albums of family photos, it isn't unusual to find, amongst those black pages and attached by silver photo mounting corners, photographs of the deceased. Children especially, laid out in their best Sunday finery, enduring the first waves of mourning. My cousin, who has one of those odd little photo albums, showed me the long-dead child that relatives say my daughter takes after. It was eerie, friends, I won't lie to you about that.

I have often wondered if there is a deeper purpose to all this careful attention—the covering of mirrors, the habit of not speaking the name but only referring to them as Mother or Sister, the grave-tending. Do we lavish this love and attention on their resting places out of a sense of duty and affection? Or are we keeping our focus there to keep them there so we don't have to treat with the perambulating dead?

The dead do sometimes return to let us know things, to impart knowledge that the living need and that was lost when the person passed on. There are tales of the deceased who appear as they looked in life—so life-like, in fact, that the living person being visited doesn't know the visitor is dead. There are stories of ghostly appearances in particular places, of the dead pointing to or standing on a spot to draw attention to it. Sometimes the all-important family Bible is there, or some saved-up cash or that prune cake recipe that Granny never would share.

Modern people easily dismiss these as delusions of the lightly educated and superstitious. But the stories persist, rolling through the ages of families and communities, and there is often the proof of the once-lost Bible or other revealed resources and information.

Haints utilize all the senses in their need to stay in touch with the world they knew. One day you may actually see one, as my sister-in-law did. This points us to the sort of ghost that doesn't seem to be aware of the living humans who now occupy the places they haunt.

I was called out to a friend's place to witness the

Civil War-era soldier who paced back and forth near the barn. I didn't see that but could feel the cold line where he trod, a line confirmed by the client. She and I stood in front of the barn in the warm sunshine and chatted about the history of that area, which happened to be near where I grew up and to Bensontown. I turned at one point to gesture up the mountain and saw a thin girl in a lightweight blue dress sitting in the open door of the barn's hayloft. She leaned against the opening, gazing toward the road to town. She was unaware (or at least non-reactive) to our presence. My client didn't see her and she faded after a time. I've never found out who she was or why she waited. Like the sleeping man at Number Ten Roberts Street, she was an imprint of a life gone by.

Mr. Haney could be heard clearing his throat and we could hear that ominous thud-thud-thud-THUD down the stairs. There are smells that go along with some haint stories—cigar smoke, perfume, and baby powder. Grieving daughters have been comforted by a mother's gentle pat on the shoulder, even after Mother's death. I don't think I've ever heard of anyone tasting a ghost, but it's not outside the realm of possibility.

My cousin's husband had worked for decades in a dyeing and finishing plant back in the days when the dangerous chemicals were not closely regulated. His last years found him battling one cancer after another before he succumbed at last to brain cancer. The whole family grieved this good and funny man, even as we felt relieved that his cancer journey had ended.

The house wasn't the same without his large presence but none of us could feel him hanging around and there was some sadness there. At last, my cousin called to tell us about her dream: she was standing on the edge of a planted field and could see her late husband far out in the middle. He was working, hoeing, weeding. As she watched, he straightened his back and turned toward her. He raised his hand in a slow wave, then returned, bending, to his work. My cousin woke, grateful to have heard from him and secure in the knowledge that he was, at last, all right.

Whether it is a leftover imprint from our Scots-Irish Ancestors or a legacy of our fierce jealousy about our privacy, traditional mountain folks take a mostly laissez-faire attitude toward their invisible neighbors. We remember the good manners our grandmothers taught us and we don't go into a relationship with our Gone Befores as though we are their bosses. We tend to be respectful, which is why you are likely to be addressed as "ma'am" or "sir" regardless of your age or social status. These attitudes are helpful in treating with the Dead but they are vital in dealing with the spirits of the land, as we shall see in the next chapter.

A Peck at the Door

Mountain people are understandably cautious around wandering spirits. A knock on the door without a visible person knocking will raise the hair right up on mountain folks. It can be a sign of impending death in the extended family. But, lordamercy, if you hear three knocks at the door (especially the back door) or on the window pain, it is a sure sign of a haint pecking on the door to come in. Under no circumstances do you shout a friendly "Come on in!"

Chapter Nine

The Cousins: Working with Local Land Spirits, and with Critters

It is a chilly November night and my house is perfumed with the cinnamon of simmering apple butter and the tang of bleach from a load of kitchen towels drying on a rack over the heat vent. That apple-bleach combination takes me right back to the ragged little orchard above our old house in west Buncombe. I am sitting in a Sheepnose apple tree and reading a library book about the Moomin Trolls. The Moomins, and the Hobbits I met a little later, merely confirmed for me what I already knew: the green and hilly world I loved so well was peopled with all sorts of folks that lived parallel lives to my own. I didn't actually see them but I understood them to be there. Was it the influence of fairy tales in different colored books that influenced my thoughts? Or the British blood in my veins? Looking back on those years, I can't remember why I thought what I did but the feeling of all those worlds so lightly connected to my own added a rich texture to my country days. As I aged, I continued reading about these conjoined places and discovered that "little people" hold pride of place in folklore all over the globe. They have different names and stories but you need only scratch the dominant culture for faeries to come flying out.

The folk in the orchard were different from the folk in the garden and the people along the old logging roads were different still. Before too long, though, I was older and more involved in schoolwork and I forgot about those peopled and unseen worlds.

Fast forward to an adult woman with a garden, a grown child and a business based on traditional Appalachian folk magic. I have research skills and language on my side and I know how to talk about these phenomena in ways that honor that near-feral child while shining some light on the notion of land spirits and how we coexist in this big and multi-layered world.

This is based on my personal experience on land that my people have been on for many generations. Your mileage, as they say, may vary. I walk easily in this place where we weave the worlds together, and I may write of it as though it is the most natural thing in the world, because for me and folks like me, it is.

Coming into a relationship may well be the theme for this work. If you have an expectation of luring in land spirits and making them do your bidding, you will find yourself disappointed. But if you wish to have a deeper kinship to all the interlocking worlds around you and to ken things that others may not, taking the time to build a relationship is well worth the effort. You can spend time with these tricksters, these wise and wild children and learn what they are willing to teach. We will look at some techniques and some tools for your work-basket. But first we are going back across the blue road of the ocean to the British Isles and to Ireland.

They still speak of it there—as we do here—with a kind of hushed reverence, tinged with awe. It seems to run down through families, this thing we call the Sight or Second Sight. It is the ability to see or to know things that are happening at a distance, a distance of either space or time. The Sight is a kind of window into other places and other times. What it means for the one who has it is bearing the ability to know aspects of life that haven't yet happened and to also know events that are happening far away from where the bearer is set. It is a double-edged gift, as most of these things are—it generally comes upon the bearer unexpectedly, in a rush of harsh and unexpected knowledge.

Those who bear the Sight also seem to have a particular link to the world of unseen folks, which is why I mention it here. In fact, people who bear the Sight were often described as "fey," which signifies their connection to the Fair Folk. If you are graced with this peculiar ability, learning your way in the world of land spirits and Guardians will be easier for you but it may also prove burdensome and require you to experience and carry grief that isn't really yours. But it is an abiding connection—one which words have no power to express. It is a blessing and a heavy obligation.

And so we return to the southern highlands, holding this strong link with our Ancestors over the water, to look at these Folks who share our mountains with us. I think of and refer to these land spirits collectively as The Cousins. The Cherokee call them the Nunnehi. My British Ancestors never referred to them by name but called them The Fair Folk or The Gentry or The Other Crowd. (Eddie Lenihan's book *Meeting the Other Crowd* is full of information and tales from that corner of the world.) There is a separate group of folks that I call the Guardians and I will tell you what I know of them, too.

Here's what I know from my experience with the Hidden People who live around and with me:

They like shiny bits and the sound of bells. They like super-sweet candies and I have found they have a preference for gummi candies in many shapes and in bright colors. Some friends ordered me some gummi candies that are shaped like chicken feet and the Folk that live in the hedge at the Italian garden love them to the point of giddiness. They also seem to enjoy spent shotgun shells and certainly love alcohol. I have found that they are less likely to accept more natural gifts—pinecones, moss and such—because they are surrounded by things like that and they don't seem special, don't seem like treats. The exception is if these gifts come from a child. They love any gifts from children.

They can be tempted to spend time with you if you give them these kinds of gifts, regularly, in the same location. Sometimes they will come to watch you work in the garden and sometimes they will help you, which means they will hinder your progress by hiding the cultivator or stealing the carrot seeds.

They like thorns. They like you to grab thorny plants that you thought were safe and they like to hear you cuss up a storm. You will feel the air around you lighten and brighten when they are present and feeling jolly.

If there is yellow nutsedge (cyperus esculentus) on your land, the Hidden Folk are there, too. It is an odd and very old plant, one of the oldest cultivated ones. They are also frequent visitors to American chestnut trees, if you are lucky enough to know one of those. They appreciate toys and find delight in black walnut shells that have been broken open and emptied of their meats. They like to torment cats.

You can conjure with them, though it is tricky. You cannot boss them around but you can cajole them and they know more about the natural world and its real and true workings than you ever will. If you treat them like friends or playmates, you will be delighted with the arrangement and the trickery will be playful and not malicious. They are good neighbors, too. If you need their help, they are willing to hear you out and consider what you need.

A few years ago, I made this thing I call a parlay stick. It was a branch of rue that had dried after I'd pulled the leaves free to make rue oil. I wrapped some of the branches in cotton embroidery thread and added some small bells. I set it up when I want to engage with the Folk and I offer some treats. Then I wait because time for them is not like time with us, which is an important thing to understand.

To do this work, you must consciously enter into a relationship based on mutual curiosity, with no fear. Think of it as hanging out, of being in a relationship where no one bosses the other being around. They are our guests and we are likewise theirs and each of our senses can be activated by our shadow guests to bring us comfort or knowledge. Many people report another avenue for communing with them—the world and language of dreams.

I have created some spirit-drawing water, that works for the Hidden People as well as Ancestors and have copied that receipt over for you at the end of this chapter.

In the last five years or so, I have begun experiencing a different set of folks, the ones I refer to as Guardians. They seem to be enormous as well as ancient and don't seem aware of us at all. They travel along fence lines and rivers and old roads. They travel slowly, as though they are very heavy. They can sometimes be spotted during thunder-and-lightning storms at night. I have seen them three times out in the mountains and I believe I heard them moving in middle Tennessee at a festival. I don't have much more information than that and am continuing my own research on these Good Neighbors.

Animals

Our Ancestors knew how and when the weather was changing and they depended on that knowledge of their environment for survival. If deer ate the kitchen garden, it wasn't a shame—it was a disaster. They couldn't take their recycled bags to the grocery store and buy what didn't grow. They spent long, exhausting days canning and preserving the food they grew and the animals they raised because without them the winter here in the southern highlands would have been very long and very lean. They depended on the knowledge that was passed down to them from the generation before and they trusted all they had learned about the fickleness of Mother Nature.

Appalachian people try not to be sentimental about the animals that are part of the world around them. If you raise animals for meat, it is wise to not get attached to them as personalities. It is a little different for milk cows and plow animals like horses and mules because you are going to be with them for a good long time. Same with dogs and cats but the modern notion of those as your "fur babies" would be laughable to people who can't do all they want for their actual babies. And the notion that you would keep any animal alive by extreme measures and with a hefty price tag is likewise difficult for anyone to understand whose money barely covers the necessities of living.

Mountain people do not have notions about "totem" animals or "spirit animals" that guide their lives. Remember these people are Protestant Bible-believers and that would seem devilish and foreign to most people, even if they admired the animals for various traits and for their beauty as God's creatures.

When I was growing up—and this happens today, too—country people supplemented what they grew and raised with wild game. Deer, rabbit, squirrel, possum, turkey, freshwater fish, groundhog. I hear that raccoon is also eaten but I remember people didn't choose that when I was growing up—eating raccoon would have been a last resort or a lucky opportunity. Bear is and was eaten but bear hunters are a different breed of hunter and when I was small, they were rare. My Uncle Horace was a bear hunter but my mother disdained the idea of eating bear meat, which was lucky for us because she was a terrible cook. Bear meat requires gentle and focused preparation and I cannot imagine how awful that would have been, served up by my mother's hands. I am shuddering just thinking about it.

Now we have wild boar up in the high country and some folks hunt that, but that is not something I remember coming up. If people wanted pork, they raised a piglet to a hog, killed it at the appropriate time, and preserved the meat in various ways.

Just as you did not pick up a book on folk magic to learn about traditional Appalachian agriculture, you are probably more interested in the magic around these wild animals so let us turn our thoughts there. Country people will watch domesticated animals for weather omens and general signs and some of those are listed in the final chapter of this book.

We'll start with snakes, which mountain people generally fear to the point of hatred. Black snakes—sometimes called black racers—are often left in peace because they are good mouse and rat eaters, and have been known to eat a poisonous snake, too. They are tolerated and seen as good thing, but most people don't want them in the house. They will also steal eggs from the henhouse so have a care about possible entry holes.

The other snakes we want to peek at are water moccasins and copperheads. Water moccasins are generally referred to as "cottonmouths" because of the color contrast between their light mouths and darker skins. They are in the pit viper family and I grew up thinking they could bite you under water—which is a good way to keep kids that can't swim out of the water. They can't, of course, and they are generally easygoing, if they aren't messed with. They will warn you—as a rattler will—by opening their very white mouth wide. Best to heed that warning. To see a cottonmouth is a foreboding sign of danger to kith or kindred, and the information is best shared so that it can be determined whom the warning is for.

We always think of copperheads as "ill" which is mean-natured and temperamental. They are beautiful snakes and they now range into suburbs and cities so finding out what they look like and how to avoid annoying them is a very good thing. We have a local Nature Center where you can safely visit our native poisonous snakes and get a good imprint in your mind about their appearance. When I was a kid, I was told again and again about their triangle-shaped heads but it seemed to me all snakes had triangle-shaped heads, even the little green ones I played with. But seeing a pit viper up close, you will notice that the jaws are immensely powerful. They smell like cucumbers, oddly enough. I remember walking into a pretty little glade up on the mountain where I lived. I stopped to catch my breath and when I inhaled, it was all cucumbers. You can bet I turned on my heel and went on another path up to the bald patch on the top. Because I was born at night, but it wasn't last night.

I might as well mention rattlers while we're here. Unlike copperheads that give you no warning and whose bite isn't too fearsome, a North Carolina timber rattler (crotalus horridus) is a burly feller, stout and ready to rattle you a warning and sometimes hiss like a cat. And if you don't pay heed, he will give you a bite or two or three that you will never forget. Both copperheads and rattlers are believed to be a sign of impending misfortune for the family of the person who sees them.

Woolly worms, on the other hand, are beloved predictors of how the upcoming winter will be, weather-wise. A solid black one means a hard winter from beginning to end. Brown at the front and the rest black means the winter will start mild but get rough. Brown on both ends means that the beginning and the end will be mild but the dead of winter will be cold and snowy. There is a Wooly Worm Festival in Banner Elk, NC in October of each year where all things woolly worm are celebrated and predictions for the coming season are pondered. There is also a woolly worm race, which is charming.

As you read in the first book, birds are often seen

as omen bringers from other places, messengers from either the spirit realm or from Heaven. I'll share a few of their properties here.

Turkey buzzards are as ugly as sin but to see them means good luck and a good crop for the year.

I do not like robins and I don't know why. Robins gathering in great numbers in your yard before any sign of spring is believed to be an omen of bad weather coming. But a single robin means that spring is here.

Dear old crows are clever and funny, but they will do damage to your garden so finding ways to keep them out of there is smart—scarecrows and aluminum-foil pie pans on strings sometimes work. Crows sometimes get a bad rap from mountain folk but they always bring me information. I keep an eye out for them. If they fly in front of me from right to left, it means everything is okey-dokey. But the opposite direction means I should be careful.

The cardinal is the state bird of North Carolina and the darling of Christmas card illustrators. Cardinals bring word from the dead, especially the recently deceased. They often arrive soon after a death to let the grieving family know that Mother is gone and is happy. The red-headed woodpecker does the same in some families. It may be that red, the color of life, is the bridge between the world of the living and the place of the dead.

The red-tail hawk is a predator, to be sure, and will happily eat an unprotected hen outside her chicken tractor. But they also are a reminder that we are looked after "from above," that powers bigger than our own have us in their view. It's a kind reminder when things are tough that you are not alone or unaided.

Whip-poor-wills used to cry their mournful song in the woods outside our kitchen door. On warm summer nights when we'd leave the door open into the evening, we'd hear the "whip, poor Will" and shudder. That call always reminds us that we are not alone and that not all spirits rest easy.

I'm going to finish here with a tale of homebrew and rummy in my cousin Evvie's basement. My mother and her cousin (who was also her best friend) were sipping homebrew and playing 500 Rummy for which there were serious rules. I'm sure my dad and Evvie's husband Whitey were around somewhere, maybe bottling up that homebrew. My brother, my cousin and myself were running around like the little heatherns that we were as the evening deepened. At one point, we heard a stage whisper from the area of the card table and we ran over. There was a large Luna moth outside on the window, attracted by the light in the growing darkness. I remember Evvie was transfixed and we all spoke in whispers. "That's grandmaw looking to see if we're okay." Well, my grandmas on both sides were still very much alive so I wondered how they turned into big green moths and came to visit. But then my sensible mother spoke and solved the riddle for me. "Grandma Westmoreland." She and Evvie nodded at each other, looked at the moth and returned to their cards.

Smoky Mountain Spirit Drawing Water

In a canning jar, combine equal parts corn liquor, spring water, hard cider. Shake vigorously and pour into a small spray bottle. Spray it on your Ancestor altar, on the gravestones in your family plot and on food you are offering land spirits or your Ancestors. Shake well before using.

Chapter Ten

Banes and Worts—Some Sovereign Remedies in Tricky Situations

This is one of the most fraught and controversial parts of what I, and many other traditional rootworkers, do. The criticism comes from all sides. You will find yourself reprimanded by members of the Pagan community who follow "the law of return" or the "three-fold law" that constrains them from putting anything they deem negative into their universe. You will be confounded by people who will insist that you are putting dangerous ideas into the hands of people who shouldn't be trusted with the responsibility. And you will be chastised, usually behind your back, by people who knew you were evil all along. This subject deserves a book of its own and may get one. But I don't think it's fair of me to claim to talk about advanced practice without addressing the issue of banework.

Hexwork. Curses. I hope this chapter will give you an idea of the sort of banework possible in Appalachian folk magic. You'll see that it is different from Afro-Caribbean banework but this comes out of my cultural tradition, for the most part, with a "borry" here and there. I find it always helpful to begin by defining terms. Then we'll have a little history and technique.

I use the word bane to mean any working intended to mitigate the actions of another. This crosses a line for some people simply because they don't cotton to the idea of interfering with other peoples' destinies. As we discussed in the section on needs/justice, there are times when we have little real recourse to the justice system and find ourselves in a place where we want a bit more input. Its origins are early, linguistically speaking, before 1000, and go back to some interesting sources in tribal Europe: it is English, from the Old English *bana* (slayer). It is cognate with Old Norse *bani* (death, murderer), with Old Frisian *bona* (murder), with Old Saxon *bano* (murderer), with Old High German *bano* (slayer), *bana* (death); akin to Old English *benn*, to Gothic *banja* wound. Definition—a source of harm or ruin. Oxford English Dictionary. Get one.

A curse is a prayer or invocation for harm or injury to come upon one. It is asking someone else, generally a divinity or spirit being of some sort, to do the damage. It comes from Old English cursian to curse, "an appeal to some supernatural power to inflict evil on someone."

When you are doing the work yourself, from start to finish, I refer to it as a hex. That is from German *hexen* ("to hex"): to bring or wish bad luck to. It illustrates one of the root sources of Appalachian folk magic in the Pennsylvania "Dutch" hexen and pow-wow traditions. I use bane for the overall category of working and then break it down according to who is actually doing the work.

Energy workings of this kind are often reduced to the unhelpful simplicity of "white" or "black" magic. I don't use the phrase "black magic" because it is too easy to make a racist jump, to be reactionary, and to create a good/bad binary. If we have to have a binary and link ourselves to such a system, I'd prefer worts and banes. Think of worts as a healthful working, a blessing. We know wort from the helpful herbs we've already engaged—mugwort used for dreams, motherwort used for connection to the Goddesses.

Much of this book and the previous one are about finding authentic practices and then practicing them. Modern Pagans are drawn to notions of authenticity and what makes something really real. That's why we get lured into aspects of cultural appropriation that temporarily meet our needs but are ultimately unsatisfying. But if we set up too strict parameters for what we will and won't accept, then we also set up roadblocks to our learning. You may choose from your own ethical base to never do any banework, but it is still a good idea to learn the history and techniques, as well as the reasoning behind their enduring legacy before you make up your mind.

And while we're touching on the concept of ethics,

let's review the sticking points of three-fold law and karma, two concepts that may be poorly understood by many people. I treat banework as a radical or extreme form of healing and see it as a way to have some effect on a situation that touches you but that you can't fix. It is how oppressed people have affected their betters and abusers for centuries. When there is no hope of law or church or justice, you use a bane. And you prepare the ground before you begin.

Here's how:

Be exact. Think it all the way through and you may choose to do nothing at all.

Be a scientist, be detached and curious. Experiment.

You will always be best served by doing this work with a cool head, not angry or vengeful. Remember, attitude is everything in this work.

Some of you will be followers of the law of attraction and will have difficulties in embracing this work as a kind of healing. And some of you may get caught up in guilt and self-blame thinking that the dire situation that needs your attention is somehow deserved, that you have actually brought it on yourself. Some of you will think of your karma and another's destiny and may ask yourself, "Why should I interfere with that? Shouldn't I let karma take its course?" For the most part, we in the west have an inadequate understanding of karma and I invite you to do some study on the complexities of the concept as reflected in Asian philosophy.

Years ago, I was struck with the axiom if you can't hex, you can't heal. I began thinking of and researching these older systems, primarily the one I have inherited here in the southern highlands. And I now see hexing as part of a continuum of healing, like cauterizing or amputation. In the interest of teaching people new to these concepts, I break banework down into levels.

Nine Levels of Bane

1. Ignore and hope it goes away. This is non-engagement. You may hear someone say that they are not feeding the particular issue any of their energy.

2. Send "good energy" is self-explanatory, I suppose. You ground yourself, access healing energy from the bosom of the Earth and send it to the one who needs it. You could use the Silver Thread or another method that works for you.

3. Set shields for personal protection, and keep them up when need be.

4. Set wards to protect more than your physical self, to protect family and property.

5. Reversal—sending the energy back to its source. Mirror work is excellent for this, whether you use an actual mirror as part of the meditation or raise mirrored energetic shields. Your intention should be strong and unambivalent: this for the one who has

harmed me, or may your actions return to you ten-fold. Let the suffering intended for me be visited upon the perpetrator. This is the first level at which you engage the malevolence directly.

6. Binding. There are several techniques for suppressing the actions of another and the easiest is by binding. Let me be clear. You are not binding yourself to the person you are focusing on. You are binding them against the habits or intentions that you want stopped. You can bind yourself, too. If you want to stop smoking or biting your nails, you can do a binding spell to help you on your way.

7. Banishing is exactly what it sounds like. The object of your focus is energetically "disappeared" to you. You will no longer feel their influence—for good or ill. It will be as if they never existed. This doesn't stop their actions but it does mitigate their effect on you and yours. I liken this to cauterizing a wound.

8. Direct Engagement. I call this a Hex and I compare it to amputation. It should have a direct effect on the subject being hexed. You may have been pretty stealthy about your banework up to this point but in this sort of working, you will reveal yourself. This is a "cease and desist or else" working, that is similar to removing a diseased limb in order to save a life.

9. A Bane is the final level, the killing curse. I have never done one and have only a little idea how I'd go

about it. But I believe it important to have as a last resort. It is the classical malediction, the thing outsiders most fear from the work-basket of folks like us. I doubt anyone could do such a curse without accruing some enormous baggage, but I suspect most of us can imagine a situation where we would risk anything to stop the miscreant or avenge a terrible wrong. As a healing modality, you may think of it as euthanasia.

You should evaluate the situation and decide what level of work is required. The numeration does not indicate a hierarchy but the levels of energy required to accomplish your task, as well as the level of control you expect to exert on your subject.

As you know, this work is not necessarily tied to any sort of spiritual system. If you choose to combine it with your ritual practice, pray or give an offering to your Divines, to the spirits of the land and to your Ancestors, in whatever way you usually do offerings of thanks and gratitude. Let me reiterate—there is nothing in the world that requires you to go beyond your comfort level with banework. If it feels oogey to you, don't do it. Don't let anyone else shame or guilt you into this sort of work. It must always be undertaken with a clear mind, a cheerful heart and a desire to cure a sick situation. Got that? Because attitude, as I have repeated countless times, is everything.

We discussed the use of tools in an earlier chapter

and this is a good place to remind you that all the things we'll be using in these receipts are simply tools. Your intention and your attitude are the best tools and ones that you carry with you at all times. That's why you can use all sorts of substitutes in folk magic.

Some Practical Receipts

Dollies are an ancient form of banework and you can do them several ways. A paper shape is easily drawn on thin paper and cut out. Name it for the one upon whom you are focused and scribble that name somewhere on the dolly. Write on it what you desire to achieve; cover all of it, front and back, with the spell. Let's use the example of you doing energy work in support of your commitment to stop smoking. You cut out your dolly and write your name across its middle. Then you focus your energy and intention on breaking your stubborn habit. Write something like, I will be a non-smoker! as many times as will fit on the dolly. Starting at the feet, roll the dolly up tightly into a small tube. You can burn it or bury it or stick it in the freezer for a Moon cycle.

A cloth dolly takes more effort but is often just the thing. Cut two pieces of plain cotton muslin and stitch them together by hand, leaving an opening along one side. Stuff the dolly with powerful herbs, either dry or fresh. Dolly herbs I use are vervain, rue and a bit of mountain mint. The cloth dolly can also be burned or buried, after it has frozen for a Moon.

Paper hexes are also traditional and easy to create. They are usually made with brown paper (paper bag paper) or with a strip from a Sears catalog. (There are so many uses for that, aren't there?) Lay the paper flat and put a stout dot in the center of it. I use a soft pencil but you can also use a Sharpie marker. Press the dot with your thumb as you set the working. "I won't be a smoker anymore!" These paper hexes can be folded into a tidy square, sachet style, or folded like the paper footballs we used to do in school. You can burn these in a little burning bowl and scatter the cooled ashes to the wind. There is more on the uses of these paper sachets in Chapter Eleven.

At a conference several years ago, one of the presenters did a talk on the northern Indian practice of creating kolam. Each morning, the woman of the house goes out her front door with colored rice flour and she creates a beautiful geometric shape, like a mandala, in the street in front of her house. Her intention is to feed as many creatures as she can, every day. Insects eat the rice, as do passing critters of all sorts and by doing so, bring prosperity into the house. By the end of the day, the last of the rice flour is scattered by the wind and the space is clear for her to do the same thing again the next morning.

This inspired me to create the Marshmallow Hex. It's

designed to cut an arrogant person down to size, and to feed some critters. Take a plain marshmallow and write the person's name upon it. Soft pencil is best for this. Once the writing is done, pierce the marshmallow with small sticks, with thorns or toothpicks. Place it out in nature where the ants can nibble it away, bit by bit. Please place it high in the crotch of a tree limb so that rambling dogs don't choke on it. Squirrels seem to nibble around the toothpicks and they won't affect insects. Safe hexing is effective hexing.

Mirror work is traditional in Appalachian folk magic. This technique is good for those low-level banes. If you are feeling set upon, sit quietly with a mirror in your hand. Look at yourself calmly, without judgment. Try to sense the energy that you feel directed toward you. Think to yourself or say aloud—back to you. Repeat that twice more as you slowly turn the mirror away from you, so that the reflective surface is facing out. Rise from your seated position and turn in a slow circle, always keeping the mirror facing outward.

No More Star Power. I continue to experiment with materials and styles of workings. Recently, I worked with star anise as an ingredient. My colleague and I picked a star anise pod for each person and passed it back and forth while discussing the person's misdeeds and determining what the best course of action was. That way we imprinted each pod with a particular person's energetic signature, as we intuited it. It was also emblematic of their particular "star power." Then we threw them all into a mortar and ground and pounded them with the pestle. We had a baking sheet and spread the powdered remains of their self-esteem/career/power on it. Then we dressed birthday candles with rue oil, one for each person. We placed some of their power crumbles inside a foil muffin cup and lined all the cups up on the baking sheet. We lit each candle and stuck them with wax into the cups. As the candles burned down, we did egg bindings on each one. By the time all the wrapping was finished, the candles were mostly done. One remained for a long, long time and we are curious to see if that person will withstand it a little longer or if he will flame out in a blaze! We did not write the names on those cups so we aren't sure which was which. We'll be sure to do that the next time we're doing such a big working. Star anise for the win!

Candle magic has been around for as long as there have been candles. Experiment with different sizes and styles for different kinds of workings. From heavy seven-day candles to tiny birthday candles, you set your intention and then you burn the candle. Simple really. I also like to dress the chosen candle with rue oil to give the working a little kick. You can do a quick working with a birthday candle in a foil cup as outlined above.

A Taste of Your Own Medicine. This working is effective for gossip, rudeness, and plain old hateful behavior. Fill a small bottle with vinegar or lemon juice. Place three black peppercorns in it and add a tiny metal nail or brad. Write the person's name on a slip of paper and roll it up, as you roll up a dolly, and place it into the bottle. Put a cork in or the lid on the bottle and seal it closed with wax. Throw it into rapidly running water—a river or large creek—or bury it off your property.

Chicken feet are not traditional to hillfolks' hoodoo but are so handy and effective that I have borried them from the techniques of the deeper South. You can allow them to dry outdoors in dry weather or you can sink them into a pot of salt to dry them out. I use them to scratch away at stubborn energies that I can't shift with bell ringing or vinegar spray and I have used them to "scratch back" against those people, entities, or energies that would harm me or mine. Several years ago, a friend also gave me some squirrel feet—a much more Appalachian possibility. I use them the same way. Chicken feet can also be hung up for protection and those little squirrel feet have gone into workings that required swift movement and a little swirl of chaotic energy.

We touched on some worts above but I want to dig a little more deeply into that little patch.

My maternal great-grandmother was a spinner. Her

wheel was left in the attic of the Knight Place house when my grandmother and mother moved from there to their next place. She raised nine children to adulthood and I don't know if there were stillbirths or miscarriages because people didn't talk about that. I do know that she also sewed—by hand and on a treadle machine. That machine, by the way, is the one I learned to sew on, too, and is currently in use as the base of one of my home altars. The women of my mother's family have a long tradition of needlework and handwork. Some of the aunties tatted, some crocheted, some did embroidery—bright slashes of color that enlivened their simple, hard lives.

I have recently taken up the drop spindle and it is frustrating but also meditative. It is called a drop spindle for a reason: when you are learning the touch of it, you are likely to spin too thin a yarn and have it twist and break. Crash goes the spindle and back you go to reattach the yarn to the pile of combed wool you are spinning (called roving) and begin again.

I am sharing this as an introduction to handmade worts, of working blessings for healing, luck, advancement into a piece of fiber art. Many religious traditions have knitting ministries where a group of people comes together for a sick congregant and the knit prayers into a shawl or small blanket. They take turns doing it and it is a companionable healing activity for the prayers as well as the recipient of the shawl.

Remember those little square potholder looms? You can still find them and if you've a mind to, you ought to pick one up (along with a bag of those loops) and make a Woven Cooking Wort. Here's what I do: I put all of the loops where they can charge in the moonlight from a waxing Moon. Then I sort those loops by color and decide which colors I prefer for the working. I always choose green and blue for healing and red/yellow/orange for jump-starting a project (perfect for a beginner cook or trying a tricky recipe). Sit with the loops in your hand and roll them through your fingers as you study the intention and the desired effect. Keep this up as long as you feel you need to and them set up the loom and weave the little square. The whole time you're weaving, be firmly putting your intention into the square. Singing or chanting it in works well, too. You may find yourself swaying in your chair as you weave. Attach a little note to it and give it to the person for whom it was intended.

A few years ago, when I worked in a bookshop and often made talks to clubs in the area, there was a book called *The Lace Reader* by Brunonia Barry. I recommend it, by the way. I went to a women's luncheon to talk about the book and the idea of scrying. One of the women had brought a basketful of handmade lace pieces and the talk ended with each woman placing a piece of lace on her dark pant leg or her skirt and me talking them through the techniques of scrying. Most of the women thought it was a lark and one of them got very quiet and nodded as she peered onto the lace. But it seemed like a possibility to me and I tried it later at home. In the spirit of handmade worts, I suggest you get a piece of handmade lace—tatted lace works fine. Place it on a second piece of dark fabric or paper and rest your hands lightly upon it. Ground yourself and breathe into a gentle relaxed state. Look at the lace before you and follow some of the threads of the pattern, if it is visible. Weave your breathing into the movement of the thread and imagine the person who created it, who made beauty in form and function. Now unfocus your eyes (or take off your glasses) and let your eyes rest on the lace. Don't follow the threads with your eyes but trace the pattern with your fingertips. Breathe deeply and slowly. Let the thoughts and images float into your consciousness and don't analyze them. When you have enough images to consider, lift your hands from the lace and focus your eyes again. Consider the images as you would dream imagery and see what you've learned.

A wort is a blessing. You may lightly touch the doorframe of any place you enter and send the people who enter there a bright blessing. Food that is cooked for potlucks can be blessed with good health for those who grew and prepared the food, as well as those who eat it. Moving through a world where you carry blessings at your fingertips like faery-dust can be a very enlightening experience for the blesser as well as all who receive a sweet blessing.

A Spell for Banishing

(In some ways, banishing is the cruelest baneworking. A banishing not only creates a world in which the object to be banished no longer has agency, it creates a world in which the object never existed. Your part in this requires good attention to your words and actions for a time, until the spell catches. You must feed the working with your clear intention until it is successful.)

Here is a kind of working that facilitates a banishing. As you approach dark Moon, write the object's name on a slip of paper. Full name, nicknames, that funny name you and other close friends use for the object. Lay the paper out near your burning bowl and heap grains of rice onto the paper. The day before dark Moon, burn three grains, leaving the residue in the bowl. The day of dark Moon, burn three more grains, again leaving any residue. On new Moon, burn the final three grains then put all the residue on the naming paper, along with a photo and any burnable memorabilia. Sprinkle dried rosemary or rosemary oil on the little pile and burn it all, as you visualize the object fading until it can no longer be seen. When the burning is done, trace a circle with your finger around the bowl, moving against the Sun (counterclockwise). Do this three times then turn and walk away from the working. As you walk, shake out your hands, removing memories of the object. Never speak of the object again. When thoughts of old times and old malices come to your head, train your mind to wonder who that person was. When people who know you both mention the object's name, have no recognition. If you see the object, do not engage in any way, as they do not exist to you. It may take several months and your good attention but it often works to "disappear" a troublesome or toxic person from your world.

Chapter Eleven

A Whatnot Jar: Receipts, Charms and Such-Like

In the cove where I grew up, there were two neighbors who planted beauty everywhere they went. They were an elderly married couple whose granddaughter was one of my best friends. She cooked on a wood stove and planted flowers all over the yard around their log cabin home. She was one who would always try new things—as I encourage all of you to do, too—and each summer saw some unique or unusual thing. One year she got green gladioli bulbs and another year she grew green zinnias. She was annoyed the year she ordered a miniature rose only to discover that it was one of the invasive multiflora roses that grew wild on the mountain.

Her husband was a woodcrafter who built little houses that dotted the yard. Those perfect miniature houses had porches and windows and doors. He also made shelves that went into the corner of a room to hold precious and breakable things and I remember a crescent moon with a couple of shelves on it that hung on the wall.

In those old days, there were always little pretties

in the world—cat's eye marbles and ornate buttons carved from mother-of-pearl and tiny tin horseshoes from the nickel machine at the store. He took a plain jar with a screw-on lid and covered it with modeling clay. Then all those little pretties got pressed into the clay to keep them in one place where they could be pondered or admired. I don't remember if there was anything inside that jar but it was a puzzle to delight a child and I was delighted.

(I recently learned that these jars have a name and probably originated in Africa, coming here with enslaved people. They are called "folk art memory jars" and are collectible. They enjoyed a revival in the 1950s in Appalachia and that explains why there was one for me to remember from my childhood.)

This final chapter is like one of those jars. It is a collection of information—oddments as well as bit and bobs—that I'd like you to know about and can't seem to find a home for them elsewhere in this book. You will find old sayings and superstitions, some new receipts for your own use and some advice along the way, as I am wont to do.

Let's begin with remembering two other containers: the sachet and the bag. A sachet (pronounced sa-shet, with the emphasis on the first syllable) is a piece of folded paper that is often tied with string. It can hold anything that is dry and not greasy, herbs and the like. It is handy for a variety of workings and is usually carried on one's person, in a pocket or pocketbook.

Bags are usually sewn of scraps of fabric but sometimes, at least in the past, they were reused cloth tobacco pouches. They also hold all sorts of dry things and are either worn on a string around the neck or carried in a pocket.

There are three sovereign herbs that I find myself using again and again, so I have taken to calling them the Three Queens. They are mugwort, vervain and rue. If you come to me with a misery of some kind—whether emotional, physical or mental—I am likely to bring you one of these good Queens. We discussed their uses in Chapter Six, but I want to sing their praises one more time. I also want you to know that your Three Queens may be different from mine and you may have a different number, too. Find green allies that complement and enhance your work and then use them. For this sort of folk magic, it is more important to know a few herbs very well than to have a scant and informal knowledge of dozens of herbs and stones. Attitude, as well as intention, will count for more in the end than a thin comprehension of the world around you.

Some Useful Sachets

As you've already read, I often recommend mugwort for folks who can't get to sleep or whose sleep is broken. A full branch of this under the pillow is good, but I've also found that a small sachet filled with dried mugwort and carried throughout the day keeps the wearer primed for a good night's sleep.

These little paper sachets are so useful because they are so cheap and easy—and effective. I encourage my students to practice magic all the time and sachets are a simple way to do that. Let's think for a minute about the usual day at work (or at home, for that matter). You have chores to do and a list of things to accomplish. Try writing those things in the center of the paper for your sachet and spend a moment thinking about the satisfaction of getting them done. Then set your intention with a dot in the middle of the list and press your thumb upon it. Fold it up and stick it in your pocket or put it on the shelf in front of your computer monitor.

Or take one with you when you are visiting a sick or sad friend. Set a general intention for nurturing and nourishing and give the sachet to your friend as a token of your affection and continued support. See how easy it is? I bet you can think of a dozen useful ways to do this little working—ways big and small.

When you must deal with the ultimate ending of a relationship or the death of someone you love, you experience something called anticipatory grief. If you have gone through the final illness of a parent, as many people in my generation are doing right now, there is a certain amount of grieving that happens along with the process of caring for them. You think of your relationship with the person, what you will never do together and often even the most pleasurable encounters are tinged with an edge of expectation that you may never have this experience again. A sachet for opening the door to healing through anticipatory grief might contain a pinch of dried American Chestnut leaf and a sprig of rosemary. Knowing that the ending will bring a new beginning is a helpful academic exercise, but walking in the realms of the gateway between this world and the next is a primal and powerful trail. Having the aid of American Chestnut can help you remember that processes can be slow but are worth the patience and the perseverance. The reward you claim is a soul more resilient while also being more open.

Some Receipts That May Come In Handy

Go Away Staub

Anne Hathaway's cottage, in Warwickshire in England, is a real beauty. The house is beautiful but I always find myself drawn to the gardens and this one is exceptional. They had some period bird-scaring machines that I adapted for banework. Here is a working to send someone on his way—bad neighbor, insistent trespasser or similar miscreants. Collect a handful of feathers—jay, crow, chicken—and get a smallish potato. Push a hole through the center of the potato with a skewer. Take a two-foot length of binding twine and run it through the potato, tying the ends together to form a loop. Choose a fine and stout staub. Drive it into the ground at an angle and nail the binding twine to the top of the staub so that your potato flies free. Now stick the feathers, one by one, into the potato. With each feather think about how happy the person will be when they are far away from you and yours. Each time—feather in, go away, feather in, go away. When all your feathers are used up or your potato is full, give it a push and a final "go away!" Each time you walk past it, set it to swinging again. Now, obviously, this is not traditional…but it could be.

Reese's Cup Power Spell

This little working came from my Candy Magic

workshop and it's a keeper. Get a Reese's Cup. The size should be determined by how big the problem is. This person is dissing you and you are going to take away his power. Not his responsibility but his power. You take the tip of a knife and carve the name into the flat top of the Cup. Then you state your intention, then peel away and devour that person's power. Peel the top of the Cup away as whole as you can. You can even cut it off with the aforementioned knife. And then put it in your mouth and let it melt away. Then peel away the sides and do the same, the whole time holding your intention. Then eat the bottom and all you're left with is the peanut center. Chill it, if need be, and then roll it into a ball in your hands. Pop that into your mouth as you thank the Earth for Her bounty and for the swift completion of the working.

Sweet Smoke

Equal parts of the following dried herbs (I'd start with one tablespoon each):

Mugwort (Artemisia vulgaris)

Rabbit Tobacco (Gnaphalium obtusifolium)

Mountain Mint (Pycnanthemum virginiana)

Put the leaves in one palm and mash them with the thumb of your other hand, releasing the oils. You can burn them on a charcoal round or put them in a burning bowl as you would white sage. Or put it in a stout old corncob pipe and smoke it. Best not to inhale this blend—some folks react badly to it—let the pipe do the work. I'm not a smoker, so the charcoal disc method is the one I prefer. Adjust the ratio to add more of the scents you like. I always go a little heavy on the rabbit tobacco. Use this as a room-cleansing smudge or to cleanse yourself or your tools.

Mountain Do (Appalachian Cleansing Water): apple honeysuckle, pine, smoke

Most everybody likes Florida water, that richly-scented toilet water that is used throughout the South for cleansing work. It is not traditional to Appalachian folk magic but I felt I wanted something similar in my little work-basket. I worked for something a little less scented than traditional Florida water and something that used the materials I work with all the time.

I call it Mountain Do and it is an Appalachian Cleansing and Blessing Water. You can easily make your own, with some simple ingredients. Try it for yourself and see how it works to clear the energy in a place, to anoint a head full of unhelpful thoughts, and to spritz the used car you got for a good price.

2 cups fresh spring or well water

¼ cup corn liquor

¼ cup hard apple cider

4 drops Liquid Smoke

10 drops honeysuckle essential oil

10 drops rose essential oil

Sprigs of fresh mountain mint, crushed

Mix all the liquids together. Fill a quart-sized canning jar ¾ full of mountain mint. Add the liquids in and shake well. Leave in the refrigerator for a Moon cycle. Remove, strain out the liquid and compost the mint. Keep it in a pretty bottle or a spritzer for use.

Weather-working Charm

I have been studying the old magics of the British Isles for the next phase of my Appalachian journey. I heard or read somewhere (isn't that always the way of it?) that the old timers in Cornwall are particularly good at weather-working. The folks on that coast often had the right of salvage when a ship went down on the jagged rocks and the goods floated ashore. And sometimes they chose to help that process along by bringing a good strong wind and a driving rain. The working I heard was a half of an eggshell in the palm of the hand. In the shell was some alcohol (scrumpy is the hard cider of that fair land), some vervain and a gob of spit. The thumb of your right hand is inserted into the egg and you turn your thumb to make the shell spin, to wind the spell and call the wind.

I was teaching an outdoor workshop and brought this up as an interesting bit of folk magic. I didn't have any of the tools and was simply miming as I told the story. It took me a few minutes to notice that the people sitting in the front row had gotten very big-eyed all of a sudden. I stopped talking to peer at them and we all felt the barometric pressure…shift. Turning to look behind me, I saw that they were all staring at the enormous dark cloudbank that was flowing up the horizon toward us. I finished up the workshop before the storm hit but it was a big blow. Pop-up tents went everywhere and some merchandise got very wet. Throughout the rest of the festival, people kept blaming me for the storm.

Now, honestly, I don't think I called that storm and I don't take credit for it. But that tale has preceded me to other festivals and when I start to tell the story of the Cornish weather-working, folks take to whispering and looking around nervously.

But, shoo, if I could really do that, I'd be out in California doing all I could to help with that terrible drought. Wouldn't you?

Some Pretties for that Jar of Yours

Mountain people are full of stories and advice and charms that guide our everyday lives. Some of these are common enough sayings that are passed down generation to generation. I've heard all of these at one time or another—and some of them I even hold to myself. Ask anyone who's ever seen me react when they tossed a hat on the bed. I've divided these up into categories: Bad luck/good luck, Omens and Admonitions, and Healing Powers.

Bad Luck/Good Luck

- Always go in the same door you went out or you'll be unlucky.
- It's also unlucky to put shoes on the table or hats on the bed.
- A buckeye in the pocket aids your good luck.
- It is bad luck to bring a digging tool—a shovel or hoe—into the house. You will be digging a grave with it.
- It is bad luck to sing while sitting at the table or to cut cornbread with a knife.
- If you open an umbrella in the house, you are tempting a lightning strike.

Omens and Admonitions

- When fog is rolling up the mountain, rain is fixing to roll down.
- If you wash clothes on Sunday, you wash someone out of your life.
- If your right palm itches, you're going to meet a stranger. If you're left one does, you're going to come into unexpected money. If the bottoms of your feet itch, you will walk on new (unfamiliar) land.

- If you give a knife or other sharp object as a gift, you can cut the relationship in two. Best to have them give you a penny and "buy" it from you.
- A cat in an infant's room will suck the baby's breath away.
- If your ear is itchy, someone is talking about you. Right ear means they're talking trash. Left means they're dishing out compliments. And some folks say when your nose itches, someone is talking about you.
- On the first morning in May, if you walk backward to the springhouse while looking in a mirror, you will see the person you will marry.
- If you drop a dishtowel, company is coming.
- Corn in the field should be knee high by the 4th of July in order to assure a plentiful harvest.
- When maple leaves turn up to show their white sides, it will rain soon.
- If you dream of a death, it means a wedding is in your family's future.
- Set stone walls on a waxing Moon to make sure they don't sink into the ground.
- If you tell someone about your dream before breakfast, it'll come true.
- After a death at home, the doors and windows must be opened wide and the mirrors covered so that the spirit may depart in ease.

- Never let a rocking chair rock without anyone sitting in it. It portends a death in the family.
- A tiny inchworm found on your arm is said to be measuring you for new clothes.
- Marking a baby—right out of Thomas Hardy, this one. If an animal startles a pregnant woman, she mustn't touch any part of her body or the baby will be born with a mark shaped like the thing that frightened her.
- If crows or starlings gather, it means rain.
- If you kill a snake, it won't die until sundown. If a terrapin bites you, it will also hold on until sundown. Or until lightning strikes.
- Stepping on graves disturbs the dead, and it's also considered bad manners.
- If you think you hear a knocking in the night—on the door or window—never, even as a joke, say "come in" aloud.

Healing Powers

- There are several cures for thrush in infants. It involves blowing into the baby's mouth. The seventh son of a seventh son or a child who has never seen her father can do this.
- Get rid of a fever blister by kissing a redhead.
- A cure for childhood asthma is to cut a branch from a sourgum tree that is the same height as the

sick child. Put the branch in the attic and when the child outgrows the branch, they will also outgrow asthma.

- Want to get rid of those adorable freckles? Wipe your face with a pee-soaked cloth diaper.
- Don't cut a child's hair until it is a year old. It will sap the baby's vitality.
- Warts—steal your mama's dishrag, wipe the warts thoroughly and bury it.
- Warts—wave a speckled hen over the affected area three times on three consecutive days.
- A buckeye carried in the pocket helps ward of rheumatism.

A careful study of Alexander Carmichael's Carmina Gadelica reveals that some of these, like the old butter charm, come directly from the British Isles.

As you try these receipts, you will find that some work well and quickly and some fall short. Stick the ones that work into your work-basket to use later. And those duds? Tweak them with different ingredients and adapt them to your own uses. Folkways, including magic work, are living traditions that change and evolve, like a fiddle tune can. Hillfolks' hoodoo is part of a family of Appalachian folkways that may survive as the culture it springs from fades and changes. Or it may not, if it is no longer useful to the people who have held it for so long. It is probably up to people like me to practice it and share it, if that feels right to them. But culture is a malleable thing and there are no guarantees of immortality, which is probably for the best.

Afterword

Gnarly Roots

I appreciate you all staying with me through two books on this odd subject. I continue to learn more and to teach and to wonder at all there is left to collect and archive. Each new place and each new person offers up glimpses into this world that has become mine by virtue of my place in this land.

My next step, along with continuing to teach and gather and learn, is to track these practices back to their roots, as much as that is possible. I outlined my plans for this new adventure in the paper "Gnarly Roots: Exploring the British Sources of Appalachian Folk Magic" that I presented at the 2013 Appalachian Studies Association national conference.

Information on this subject is never direct or simple, in contrast to the actual practice of these traditions. What seems to be a likely path is bisected again and again with odd trails and excursions, leading the curious folklorist to a new overlook and potentially a new way of thinking about the wheres and whens and whys of her own research.

The Appalachian mountains were inhabited for 12,000 years before the Europeans arrived and the in-migration of Scots-Irish from Ulster brought a Protestant flavor to the steep slopes and barely-arable land.

They brought with them their own folkways, which borrowed heavily from the pre-Christian traditions in their homelands. These practices were thrown into proximity to similar Cherokee and German ways to create the vibrant folk magic tradition that is enjoying a revival today. Layer after layer is sorted and stacked like boundary-marking cairns on the hilltops.

Exploring the roots of the practices that were common in the rural landscape of my childhood has shown me three primary sources—British, German and indigenous American.

European settlers began arriving in the southern highlands in the late 17th and early 18th centuries. Coming through the ports of Virginia and Maryland, the immigrants—for a variety of reasons—pushed deeper into the less occupied lands. Many of these early settlers were what have come to be called Scots-Irish—Protestant Scots from Ulster who had been planted there during the time of James I. There were also transported members of wild reiver clans from the no-man's-land of the Anglo-Scottish border, as well as settlers from the mountainous, forested lands of the German Palatinate, whose kindred brought the Hexen or pow-wow tradition into Pennsylvania. This motley band of immigrants and their own folkways came face-to-face with the indigenous peoples of the region, notably the Tsalagi—the Cherokee.

In unraveling the Irish and Scots-Irish diasporas, I have run into a group so immediately linked (and so powerfully like) the people around me in western North Carolina that I have become enmeshed in their lore, their practices and their history. My thesis is that it was the essential nature of this particular group of immigrants, their hard journey to this country and the isolation that was their lot for generations that led the southern highlands to be a fertile ground for modern Pagan religions.

I am speaking of the Moss-helmets and the Steel Bonnets—the reivers of the Anglo-Scot borders. The borders of any place become a crucible for change and expansion and that is especially true for states and nations. In that liminal place—like teeming country hedgerows—there is a collision of life and lifestyle that makes for a hybrid vigor and for culture clashes. That was true of the border between England and Scotland— an area usually referred to as the Border Marches. The counties on either side were often lawless—perhaps because jurisdiction was tricky to assign. Hadrian's Wall had marked the boundary between Roman Britain and the wild Picts to the North, but centuries later the inhabitants of the area were abused by the encroaching militias of both sides of that line.

It made for an uneasy settlement and the reivers were one of the results of a land always in play in the tug-of-war between two ancient enemies. Crops were destroyed, livestock stolen, houses and barns burned to teach a lesson to common folks who had little or no recourse to either London or Edinburgh. Out of this chaos grew the reivers who were loyal to no country— only to their families and clans. They ran sorties across the border—as Celtic tribes had done since time immemorial—and looked after their own.

When James VI also laid claim to the English throne, there was agreement at last between the two lands on one thing. The reivers had to go.

They were tried, then executed or transported into Catholic Ulster and more than a century later they removed themselves into the new world of America. For the purposes of my research, a group reliant on its wits and skills in raiding would be very likely to invoke both rugged healing techniques and protective charms for those who were riding and raiding—and for those who were left behind.

Much of what I'm finding ties in with the culture that pervades the fastnesses of the southern highlands. The notion of being loyal to no authority other than family/clan rings true for anyone who has crossed these people or has been sheltered by them in the face of injustice. I am fascinated by the nature of the border reivers and their jagged pilgrimage into western North Carolina, as viewed through the lens of my current work as an independent folklorist with my particular focus in Appalachian folk magic.

I am grateful to Sir Walter Scott and other antiquarian collectors for leading me to this unfamiliar place and to these future Appalachian folks. People who lived the sort of life that has been attributed to the border reivers would have used any possible means of protection, including charms and talismans. Likewise they would have been likely to impede the people who were gunning for them—whether English or Scots—by whatever means at their disposal, including hexes and curses.

Who were the reivers? It is tempting to conflate them with the old Celtic tribes of Britain, but their pedigrees are much more complex and interesting. Picts, the remnants of the Dal Riada, Saxons, Norsemen, Norman nobles, traders from Flanders, and more, made the inhabitants of the border marches one of the most diverse populations in mediaeval Britain.

Besides the obvious factors along the border, shifting loyalties, and near-constant physical and economic threats, there were other circumstances that led to the reiver culture's contempt for outside authority. The reivers assured their security through a Darwinian survival of the strongest and most cunning.

Estates were divided amongst all male heirs. It took only a few generations to so divide the land that no one could make a living from it. The land itself, much like the land they would later claim in the Appalachians, was hilly and the soil thin. Suited for livestock grazing but not farming, leading reiver families to collect large herds that were very portable for a raiding party from either side of the border. Most raiding occurred in late autumn and early winter, as the nights lengthened and the herds were fat from summer grazing.

Before the ascension of James I and VI, both governments alternated between punishing the border families and encouraging them in their lawlessness. After all, these experienced fighters and raiders were the first line of defense and they were often successful at turning back troops that would otherwise have invaded.

The reivers would raid—it was called "riding"—on small sure-footed horses, and were known as some of the finest cavalrymen in Europe. Upon meeting one notorious border reiver, Queen Elizabeth had quipped that with ten thousand such, James I "could shake any throne in Europe." Once captured by either Scotland or England, some reivers would serve as mercenaries in lieu of being hanged, or worse.

These transplanted border folks, along with Lowland Scots also in Ulster, made up some of the immigrants who later sought the freedom of the lands in the Americas. Their ragged migration took them into Pennsylvania and then down the Shenandoah valley of Virginia and at last into the lands so like the ones their Ancestors had departed centuries before— the rolling, forested and thin-soiled mountains of the Appalachians. They settled in and took up the shards of culture left them: the self-sufficiency, the disdain for authority, the safety of kin. They were fierce fighters still, as witnessed by their use as troops before and after the foundation of the nation. But their choice of home also kept them separate from the mainstream, isolated, eking out an existence as farmers until the more lucrative jobs of timber and coal mining were available.

The early 16th century Archbishop of Glasgow, Gavin Dunbar, was fed up with the unchurched and unwashed and uncontrollable reivers, my Ancestors. He pronounced a dramatic and terribly thorough curse on them. Part of it is carved in a boulder now on display at the Millennium Gallery in Carlisle.

"I curse them going and I curse them riding; I curse them standing and I curse them sitting; I curse them eating and I curse them drinking; I curse their wives, their children, and their servants who participate in their deeds. I curse their crops, their cattle, their wool, their sheep, their horses, their swine, their geese, their hens, and all their livestock. I curse their halls, their chambers, their kitchens, their stanchions, their barns, their cowsheds, their barnyards, their cabbage patches, their plows, their harrows, and the goods and houses that are necessary for their sustenance and welfare."

Poor old reivers.

So I am setting myself up as a wandering spell-catcher like the song-catchers that came before me. I intend to wander these backward trails in search of the tidbits, the threads that hold these cultures together and came to create the garbled and lively folk magic practiced in the southern highlands of Appalachia down to this very day. I have a mad-stone and a piece of hard mica in my pocket, and I have made some room in my work-basket for whatever practical bits and bobs I bring home. Fare you well, friends, until we meet again.

Appendix One

Tools

- burning bowl/cauldron
- a work-basket to hold your tools (retro make-up case, doctor bag: check Goodwill, yard sales, etc.)
- a collection of Mason jars with lids
- cutting tools (chopping/butcher knife, whittling knife, scissors)
- grinding tool (mortar and pestle)
- sealable plastic bags in several sizes
- baskets for drying/carrying/storage
- fire (matches, firestick)

Appendix Two

A Way of Grounding

Sit comfortably with your feet flat on the floor and your hands loose in your lap. Begin breathing, deep belly breaths. Wiggle your toes and press your feet into the floor, really feeling the connection. Drop that connection through the layers of flooring (assuming you're inside) until you feel the Earth beneath.

(I always liken this to hugging someone in a winter coat. Just because you are both wearing down jackets, it doesn't mean you can't hug another person. Same with Earth. There may be a layer of concrete and rug and wood and whatever between you and actual soil, but those are only coverings.)

Imagine the coolness of it and the damp. Feel tiny roots grow from the bottoms of your feet down into the soil. As they stretch and grow, they become fatter and stronger, until they reach deep into the crust of the Earth.

Breathe, breathe.

Now imagine that your feet are empty, nothing inside. Feel this openness travel up your calves and knees, through your thighs and hips and bottom, all the way to your belly button. Let it rest there.

Now let the energy level rise up through those open spaces and fill the lower half of your body with strong, supporting, green Earth energy.

Breathe, breathe.

Shake your hands out and roll your shoulders a bit to loosen up your upper body. Open your mouth wide and yawn. Make a sound. Connect the upper part of your body to the lower and when you feel that connection, put your hand flat against your belly button.

Wiggle your feet again, imagining that your roots are movable and that you take this rooted connection with you wherever you go. Stand and stretch upward, as though you are picking apples from a tall tree. Breathe deeply into your whole body.

On each exhale, let the energy level remain steady as you slowly fill your bottom half with this receptive, lively energy.

Breathe. Breathe.

Now visualize an opening in the top of your head and do likewise with the upper part of your body. Let the lumps and bits float out and away becoming clouds and trees and flying away, away. Your fingertips empty, your forearms, upper arms, your chest, your throat your head. Up, up and away! Now let the soft, cool, golden energy of the Moon pour down into the empty vessel of your upper body, flowing down to stop at your navel. Effortless, let it flow into you.

Breathe, dear ones.

The two energies, green and golden, cool and warm, meet in the center of your being. As they flow together, renew your grounding and feel the center of you warming and activated. (Sometimes when you get to here, your bladder gets activated, too. Word to the wise.) This combined rich energy is there at your center and ready to be utilized. As you renew your grounding, feel sharp energy come up through the backs of your legs and across your shoulders, stretching to the tips of your fingers. Feel your connection across space and time. With practice and experience, this will give you the feeling of being connected to the Universe itself, connected and powerful, an elemental force in complete control of boundless energy.

This is where focus comes in. As this connection occurs, you must bring to your conscious mind the intention for the work you are doing. Focus on it like the proverbial laser.

Breathing still, the next step will be to send your intention out on the flow of this energy.

When you come to this deeply connected and focused place, don't waste it by simply regrounding the energy and coming back into your full physical self. Keep it for your own healing, send it to a sick friend, or let it flow back into the Earth with a healing intention. Waste not, want not.

Appendix Three

The Silver Thread

Here's the protocol for the Silver Thread, sometimes called the Silver Cord, which is an old Irish healing modality for connecting over a distance. It can be used for other things than healing but I have found it very effective for that. Go to a place of meditation or into an alpha state. Imagine the tips of the fingers of your dominant hand. Feel them warming up. Imagine that a white light forms at the tips and as it projects out into a beam or thread, it turns to silver. Then you imagine that thread leaving where you are and going directly to the person you are working for. Imagine it quite literally, as far as you can. It goes down the steps and out the front door and up the street and onto the highway and...you get what I mean. When it arrives at its destination, send pulses of energy (always pulling the energy from the Earth and not out of yourself) along the thread, breathing out healing, breathing in love. Break the connection by reeling the thread back in, like a fishing line. Finish by putting your hands together, pressing them into the earth and coming back from your meditative state.

Appendix Four

Glamoury

A glamour is a spell for personal advancement of some kind. Often you will encounter a glamour in meetings where it's important to one of the participants to get the attention of (or the upper-hand on) everyone else in the room. With experience, you can sometimes smell a glamour—I'm not kidding. But if you are sitting in a group (or alone with another person) and you can't figure out why that person is getting such a sweet reception from the gathered folks, there may be a glamour at work. If you are sitting with another person and can't figure out why you are hanging on her every word, that's a glamour. It is a very old technique, very useful and often done in the most unconscious of ways. Some of them are innocent enough—when you go to court, you want the judge to see you as the injured party or as a competent witness or whatnot. But often the point of the glamour is to get ahead of people who have worked harder or are more knowledgeable than the glamour-caster.

I developed this technique for casting a glamour after mastering Laurie Cabot's "getting to alpha" working from one of her earlier books. I've used it in lots of situations, from auditioning for a play to interviewing for a job.

Setting a Glamour

You will need to do a deep grounding, put up your own shields and listen to your inner guidance. A glamour is a way of presenting yourself so that you are seen and experienced exactly as you mean to be seen. That can lead to all sorts of truth-telling because you will seem like a strong and good authority.

To do a glamour, you stand looking at yourself in a mirror, shoulder and head only not full-length. You look yourself in the eyes and you begin to go over in your head exactly how you want to appear. Once you have a little mantra down—strong, sane, reasonable, righteous (whatever your key words are)—you begin to tap with the middle finger of your non-dominant hand into the center of the palm of your dominant hand. Tap tap tap.

Keep looking at yourself, tapping, repeating the words (either aloud or silently).

You will feel a sensation, cool for some, warm for others, that starts at your ankles and works its way up your body. Usually it centers on your face.

When it gets to your face, repeat the phrase one last time and add *Yes, just like that*. Then stop tapping. If you don't get that sensation, keep up the tapping et al.

until you feel "full." That means the glamour has set.

And if you get all flustered when you are in the place where you need the glamour to hold, simply reground and do the tapping again, surreptitiously. That recharges the glamour.

Busting a Glamour

Ground yourself and start listening and smelling. Start deep breathing to clear your energy field. When you are ready to start, simply sit with your forearms resting on your thighs. Open up your left hand, palm-up—and begin tapping the center of that palm with the middle finger of your right hand. You'll start to feel the one hand get warm and then the other. When the energy feels to be flowing back and forth between the tapping hand and the receiving hand, look up at the person you believe is "glamoured." No need to glare or give them the stink-eye—simply let your eyes rest upon them and keep tapping. Soon you will be rewarded with seeing the person as they really are—tired, shaky, afraid, and nervous. If you want to expose the glamour to the other people assembled, give a little nod of thanks and keep tapping. Listen and feel the shifting of energies in the room. You may be rewarded with seeing the whole crazy house of cards come tumbling down.

Appendix Five
Seven Herbs Seasonal Cycle

Since learning the beautiful "Seven Herbs of Spring" song from our Beloved Crone Antiga, I've been playing around with my favorite magical plants for each season. I did fall first, then added the other two seasons. These are the ones I love—please take a look at them and note which ones are your favorites for each season. Many of them are available in more than one season— mugwort and parsley, for instance, are available in every season. Here for your consideration is the Seven Herbs Seasonal Cycle.

Winter

Hellebore, witch hazel, ivy, holly, pine, ground cedar, rowan

Spring

Nettle, chickweed, plantain, dandelion, ramps, violet, sweet woodruff

Summer

Mountain mint, lemon balm, catnip, rosemary, lavender, datura, rowan

Fall

Pokeweed, gentleman's walking stick, rabbit tobacco, mugwort, vervain, rue, black walnut

Suggested Reading

These books are useful as well as good to read. This list is a fancy candy box with some fiction, some history, some practical gardening advice and a couple invite good eating. There's magic, too.

Adams, Sheila Kay. *Come Go Home with Me*

Bledsoe, Alex. *The Tufa Tales,* starting with "Hum and the Shiver." And while you're at it, check out the band Tuatha Dea.

Cavender, Anthony. *Folk Medicine in Southern Appalachia*

Deppe, Carol. *The Resilient Gardener*

Flynt, J. Wayne. *Dixie's Forgotten People*

Foxwood, Orion. *The Candle and the Crossroads*

Hartley, Dorothy. *Lost Country Life*

Kahn, Kathy. *Hillbilly Women*

Kavaya, Karol and Skemp, Vicki. *Community Quilts*

Lane, Vicki. The Elizabeth Goodweather books, starting with *Signs in the Blood*

Morrison, Dorothy. *Utterly Wicked*

Pyle, Jack, and Reese, Taylor. *Raising with the Moon*

Rago, Linda Ours. *Blackberry Cove Herbal*

Swell, Barbara. *Log Cabin Cooking*, also *Children at the Hearth* and really any of her little clever books

Thomas, Robert B., Ed. *The Old Farmer's Almanac*

Wigginton, Eliot, Ed. The Foxfire books, edited by Eliot Wigginton and his Rabun County students, starting with *The Foxfire Book*

About the Author

H. Byron Ballard, BA, MFA, is a ritualist, teacher, speaker and writer. She has served as a featured speaker and teacher at Sacred Space Conference, Pagan Unity Festival, Pagan Spirit Gathering, Southeast Wise Women's Herbal Conference, Glastonbury Goddess Conference and other gatherings.

She serves as elder priestess at Mother Grove Goddess Temple, a church devoted to the many faces of the Divine Feminine, where she teaches religious education, as well as leads rituals.

Her writings have appeared in print and electronic media. Her essays are featured in several anthologies, including "Birthed from Scorched Hearts" (Fulcrum Press), "Christmas Presence" (Catawba Press), "Women's Voices in Magic" (Megalithica Books), "Into the Great Below" and "Skalded Apples" (both from Asphodel Press). She blogs as Asheville's Village Witch (myvillagewitch.wordpress.com) and as The Village Witch for Witches and Pagans Magazine (witchesandpagans.com/The-Village-Witch), where she is also a regular columnist. Her pamphlet "Back to the Garden: a Handbook for New Pagans" has been widely distributed and her first book, *Staubs and Ditchwater: A Friendly and Useful Introduction to Hillfolks' Hoodoo* (Silver Rings Press), debuted in June 2012. Byron is currently at work on *Gnarly*

Roots: Spell-Catching and the Origins of Appalachian Folk Magic, and *Earth Works: Eight Ceremonies for a Changing Planet.*

Contact her at www.myvillagewitch.com, info@myvillagewitch.com.